Born in 1927, Roy Dean was educated at Watford Grammar School and evening classes. After serving in the RAF for three years, he handled government publicity campaigns at the Central Office of Information. He later moved to the Commonwealth Relations Office and the Diplomatic Service, which led to postings to Sri Lanka, Canada, Nigeria and the USA. As Director of the Foreign and Commonwealth Office's Arms Control and Disarmament Research Unit, he represented the UK on one of the UN Secretary General's Expert Groups, and played an important role in support of the arms control negotiations which led to the end of the Cold War. In his final posting he was acting British High Commissioner in Ghana. On retirement he started a new career as a writer and broadcaster. He wrote and presented three series of programmes for BBC Radio 4 on *The Poetry of Popular Song,* and has collected ten of his own compositions in *A Simple Songbook* (2002). He has twice won the Times National Crossword Championship and holds the world record for the fastest verified solution of the Times Crossword. He is vice-president of Bromley Arts Council.

To Joan

*With thanks
and best
wishes.*

MAINLY IN FUN

*Roy
18/11/08*

Roy Dean

The Book Guild Ltd
Sussex, England

First published in Great Britain in 2002 by
The Book Guild Ltd
25 High Street,
Lewes, East Sussex
BN7 2LU

Limited edition published in 1998 by
One Yard Press

Typesetting in Garamond by
Keyboard Services, Luton, Bedfordshire

Printed in Great Britain by
Bookcraft (Bath) Ltd, Avon

A catalogue record for this book is
available from the British Library

ISBN 1 85776 668 7

TO HEATHER

*For the fun we have enjoyed
together over fifty years*

CONTENTS

PARODIES

SPOOFS

TRANSLATIONS

BALLADES

LIGHT VERSE

CROSSWORDS

CROSSWORD AND QUIZ ANSWERS

FOREWORD

I first came across the name of Roy Dean when he won the first *Times* National Crossword Competition in 1970, from a field of 20,000 solvers. Later that year I was spectacularly impressed by his achievement in solving a *Times* puzzle on the BBC *Today* programme in 3 minutes 45 seconds, to establish a world record which remains unbeaten. Shades of Dean Swift!

I have expressed my admiration by referring to this feat in my books. Inspector Morse's endeavours to beat the record were inevitably interrupted by Sergeant Lewis, but they were always foredoomed to failure.

Although we have regularly crossed swords with each other in the *Observer*'s monthly Azed crossword competition, I was unaware that Roy was an accomplished author in his own right until he sent me some of his verse parodies. I consider 'A Shropshire Lass' nothing short of brilliant. Like him, I am a great Housman fan, and it was an added pleasure to receive his other fine parody, 'A Somerset Lad', which has been honoured by the Housman Society.

But this anthology is something else. The sheer range of subjects – crosswords, wordplay, song lyrics, international diplomacy, art, music, literature – and the various styles in which they are written would be remarkable enough; but when the dish is seasoned with wit and humour the smack is splendid.

In short, *Mainly in Fun* is a delight, full of quirky, erudite ingenuity. I had no hesitation in nominating it one of my Books of the Year in 1998, and I hope it will now find the wider readership it so richly deserves.

Colin Dexter

Oxford

WORDPLAY

It was a strange but happy chance that the names of the players in the MCC team touring South Asia in 1961/62 were ideally suited to punning. Hence these verses, published in the *Ceylon Observer* in September 1961.

ODE TO THE MCC

All followers of cricket
Salute the MCC!
Pay tribute at the wicket
To their Dexterity.

Admire the Barber's cutting,
The Pullar's hefty smite;
On runs see Parfitt glutting –
And not-so-gentle Knight.

With bat like viper flashing
See Russell guard his stumps;
What mighty Smith-like smashing,
What satisfying Crumps!

Batsmen are creased with worry
By Lock-Smith's keen attacks,
With Millman there, or Murray,
Grinding behind their backs.

Observe how Allen's finger
Sends tricky spinners down;
Would any hero linger
To face both White and Brown?

Let richness Richardsonic
Not peter out again,
And batting Barringtonic
Remain within our ken.

A Ceylonese solicitor and prolific rhymester, writing under the name of 'Gallinago' (The Snipe), responded to the foregoing ode with one of his own, published the following week in the *Ceylon Observer*. Very helpful to me in a cricket-mad country!

ODE TO THE DEAN

I don't care much for cricket,
The blooming MCC
Can play on any wicket,
It matters naught to me.

But I must confess I'm smitten
With admiration keen
For the verses that were written
By the Diplomatic Dean.

I like his lilting rhythm,
(He's a master of the pun).
My feelings were right with him
In his lively sense of fun.

He knows his Russell's Viper...
I read with great delight
His digs at every swiper
From the Barber to the Knight.

If diplomatic dealing
Were couched in poetry
I have a sneaking feeling
There'd be peace and harmony.

So, to Mr Dean, who raises
Our hopes, let's doff our hats,
And let us sing the praises
Of this Dean of Diplomats.

4

In 1963 the British pianist, Denis Matthews – a great exponent of the glories of Bach – lectured at the University of British Columbia in Vancouver. When I chatted to him he deplored the Draconian provincial laws that prevented him from getting a drink. I smuggled a bottle of Scotch to him with a musical limerick, for which he was very grateful. He replied in similar vein when he reached Montreal.

BACK TO BACH

To Denis Matthews

Bach's music soon went out of fashion,
And listeners got a poor ration.
Then Mendelssohn came
To discover his name,
And now he is D. Matthews' passion.

A NEAT RESPONSE

From Denis Matthews

Dear Roy, many thanks for your gift,
And for giving old Johann a lift;
Just as he needs no hyphen
I'll search for no syphon
To send my good spirits adrift.

My ration of passion's complete
As with Bach (& with Scotch) I'm replete;
It's so hifalutin'
To go on dilutin'
The things that are best taken neat.

IN VINO VARIETAS

In 1970 the Deinhard wine company offered a Caribbean cruise for the best limerick celebrating their Green Label Moselle. The erudite Ronald Hope-Jones (who sadly died in 2000) and I were colleagues then in the FCO Disarmament Department, and sometimes compared notes on our competition entries (written outside office hours!). He liked my rather feeble attempt:

> Said a bibulous farmer named Weller
> 'For Moselle I'm a helluva feller.
> I've stocked up my stable
> With Deinhard's Green Label –
> Now my byre is becoming a cellar!'

Ronnie's own splendid entry was:

> When last I had dinner with Mabel
> I ordered five Deinhard Green Label.
> We had two with the meat,
> And two with the sweet;
> The fifth we had under the table.

Of course, he won the coveted prize, and at the end of July he dropped a note on my desk:

> Mabel victorious,
> Tipsy, uproarious.
> Isn't it glorious!
> Here's to us all!

The following weekend we met at the final of the first *Times* National Crossword Championship, which I was fortunate enough to win. This represented an extraordinary diplomatic double within the space of a few days, crowned by a personal note from the then Foreign Secretary, Sir Alec Douglas-Home.

Some time later Ronnie and I collaborated in a newspaper competition for a crossword clue on a distinguished person, and came up with the winner: 'One put in to manage the Church (6)'. Ronnie and I tossed for it and he took the prize again!

This dinner-party game originated in Lagos in 1965 during the dark days of the Nigerian Civil War. It was featured by Hunter Davies in the *Sunday Times* as his Christmas competition that year, and drew a huge response.

THE APOSTROPHE GAME

Many languages – including our own – use the apostrophe to indicate a letter or letters omitted: '*L'Elisir d'Amore*', '*L'Après-midi d'un Faune*', for example. But English is probably unique in using the apostrophe for the possessive case; others have to employ special endings or prepositions to produce a genitive. The Apostrophe Game is designed to exploit this special quality.

The idea is that you have to take a proper name or phrase of two or more words, of which the last word begins with 'S' or the sound of 'S'. You move the 'S' forward to the end of the previous word, drop in an apostrophe, and write a clue to the sound of the new format. For example, the clue 'Elizabethan fish-fork' would lead to the answer 'William's Hake-spear', and in sport 'A hole in one' would be 'Sam's Need', and so on. There are literally thousands of possibilities.

The party hostess divides the guests into two teams. Each team presents a clue, which the other side has to guess in two minutes. Points are awarded for a correct solution, or to the presenter of the clue if it is not solved.

Here are some examples from the world of the arts:

1. Uncle Tom's breakdown . . . .
2. The lay of the last minstrel . . . .
3. A prong is a prong is a prong . . . .
4. Agony or ecstasy? . . . .
5. A quiet donnish hack . . . .
6. Shandies all round . . . .
7. Private eye rewarded . . . .
8. Warning on the beach . . . .
9. Mrs Warren . . . .

10. The Wealth of Nations . . . .
11. In the Galsworthy kitchen . . . .
12. Puritan's Indian girlfriend . . . .
13. Folk-song instrument . . . .
14. Prompt composer . . . .
15. Painted horse-troughs . . . .
16. Conductor paid in silver . . . .
17. The sounds of rock group . . . .
18. Rare pants for Axel . . . .

And here are some familiar names and phrases:

19. Down in the forest . . . .
20. First fruit of woman MP . . . .
21. For angry dramatic writing . . . .
22. Laughed away with the Pill . . . .
23. Why the British never panic . . . .
24. Big reason for changing partners? . . . .
25. Opener for Irish oarsmen . . . .
26. Supporter in bunker at St Andrews . . . .
27. Result of open-air concerts . . . .
28. Unfair advantage of college pudding . . . .
29. Why boxer can fight again . . . .
30. Cosmetic aid to Miss World trophy . . . .
31. Snooker ace in the garden . . . .
32. Gamble for a bag of soot . . . .
33. From tanker's mouth . . . .
34. Swerving ball from pub player . . . .
35. Please send me rain . . . .
36. 30 x 24, mostly wet . . . .

[Solutions on page 229]

CONVERSION TABLES

In January 1971, when the Meteorological Office was about to introduce temperatures in Centigrade in place of Fahrenheit, the publishers Methuen invited suggestions for mnemonics to help listeners to adjust to the new system.

My method is to chant a little jingle:

> From Fahrenheit to Centigrade
> A cut of thirty-two is made;
> Divide by nine to rectify,
> Then five times must you multiply.
>
> From Centigrade to Fahrenheit
> Divide by five to keep it tight;
> Then multiply by nine, and you
> Must add the sum of thirty-two.
>
> (Remember as you calculate
> That twenty equals sixty-eight).

Alternatively, if you prefer initials, you might convert from Centigrade thus:

> Fivefold Abate; Have Rest Expanded Ninefold;
> Here Enter Incremental Thirty-two.

An entry for a competition for a poem consisting entirely of two-syllable words, published in the *Spectator* in July 1983.

DISYLLABICS

Passions denied demand release;
Innate reserve cannot survive
Extreme desire. Feelings increase
Beyond relief, aflame, alive.

Therefore relent, demure princess,
Before despair becomes despite;
Unloose restraint, accept caress,
Dissolve into intense delight.

Another competition called for a line of verse in which the second half was an anagram of the first. The leading entry appeared in the *New Statesman* in April 1984.

ANAGRAM VERSE

I loved the girl, and all died overnight.

Terms of endearment, met for tender names.

Into the countryside, no city's din out there.

Ted Heath had teeth.

The first two of these entries to a competition for sporting clerihews were published in the *New Statesman* in June 1984.

SPORTING CLERIHEWS

Rugger's
A game for silly buggers
Who are prepared to risk all
For a misshapen ball.

Professional snooker
Offers lucre;
Even the dimmest of clots
Can make pots.

English Soccer's
Fair game for the mockers;
Even the mighty Beckham
Can't check 'em.

Chess
Demands great finesse;
You need less subtle crafts
For draughts.

The worst thing at cricket
Is to be lbw.
Better to go for gold
And be c & b.

Tennis is
Becoming full of menaces;
Hear the expletives flow
From McEnroe.

In a competition for clerihews on celebrities, the first of these entries was published in the *Spectator* in January 1986, and in *The Wit of the Spectator* (Century, 1989).

CELEBRITY CLERIHEWS

Mrs Mary Whitehouse
When taken to a lighthouse
Was seen to gape
In horror at its phallic shape.

Ronald Reagan
Has become a vague 'un;
How many times has he tripped
Over his script?

Whatever you think of Thatcher
Few can match 'er;
Surely her greatest feat
Was to put beggars on the street.

Although Tony Benn
Feels affinity with working men,
The chances are slim
That they feel the same about him.

Sir Edwin Lutyens
Designed several escutcheons
For members of the General Staff
He'd met at the Cenotaph.

Will Shakespeare
Should not be confused with Nick Breakspear;
One wrote plays by the score,
The other became Adrian IV.

Antonio Diabelli
Developed a beer-belly;
What with drinking and free board
He could hardly reach the keyboard.

The chief glory of the clerihew, invented by E.C. Bentley in 1905, is that the lines are of uneven length and do not scan. Perversely the clerick, invented in 1997, takes an existing clerihew, adjusts the wording to fit a metre, and adds a fifth line in the style of a limerick.

As a party game, one side recites a well-known clerihew and the other team is given five minutes to turn it into a clerick. Here are some examples.

CLERICKS

To his servant said Christopher Wren:
'I am going to dine with some men.
If anyone calls,
I'm designing St Paul's,
So please ask them to call back again'.

When that delicate bard Geoffrey Chaucer
Had to take a cold bath in a saucer,
(After several hints
Dropped by the Black Prince),
His voice became hoarser and coarser.

As a student at Cambridge John Keats,
Among other notable feats,
Drank a full soup tureen
Of the true Hippocrene,
With a plateful of various meats.

The poems of D.G. Rossetti
Were sweetly and charmingly pretty;
But the one that began
'Why d'you melt waxen man?'
Was as sloppy as soggy spaghetti.

That great English genius Purcell
Was frequently drunk at rehearsal;
But thinking it best
To take several bars rest
He achieved alcoholic dispersal.

When Spain said the works of Cervantes
Were worth half a dozen of Dante's,
The people of Italy
Resented it bitterly
And chanted Hispanophobe shanties.

As a tutor of maths Lewis Carroll
Could never afford fine apparel,
But he built a fine palace
With the profits from *Alice*,
And ordered his wine by the barrel.

On a certain occasion when Browning
Saved a debutante swimmer from drowning,
And she asked what he meant
By 'the good news from Ghent',
He replied: 'This is no time for clowning'.

This anagram quiz was devised for Bromley Art Society's Christmas party in 1990.

FIND THE PAINTER

You can discover the identities of these artists by solving the anagrams in the titles of the paintings.

1. VINDALOO AND RICE . . . .
2. CAMELOT NUDE . . . .
3. SCARF ON CABIN . . . .
4. CHANNEL TO JOBS . . . .
5. STILL NOTICE-BOARD . . . .
6. RED CURL BATHER . . . .
7. ALPACA FOR IDLE SCREEN . . . .
8. PALE LUKE . . . .
9. KID ON CHEVY AD . . . .
10. THIN ON CHIVES . . . .
11. A SADDER EGG . . . .
12. OUR EASTER EGGS . . . .
13. RAW AND HOLY . . . .
14. NEVER JAR ME
15. WHY END WATER? . . . .
16. SUGAR IN OUR TEE . . . .
17. A TANNED MANAGER . . . .
18. PLUMS ARE MEAL . . . .
19. MARINE THESIS . . . .
20. ROLL A SAD DIVA . . . .
21. PURE BILGE THERE . . . .
22. SOAP BOILS CAP . . . .
23. A LUSH NAP . . . .
24. CANNERY PESTLES . . . .
25. ICA UNFURLED . . . .

[Solutions on page 230]

15

This anagram quiz was devised for Bromley Music Society in 1991, bicentenary of the composer's death.

MOZART MEDLEY

An international group of musicians and singers have got together to celebrate Mozart's Bicentenary by giving a series of concerts featuring his works. Can you unscramble their names to find out what they are going to perform?

1. LIZZIE ANGERDOOF   . . . .
2. JULIET-SUE BATTLEAX   . . . .
3. DENIS CHEVAL   . . . .
4. CORONA COBSTONES   . . . .
5. GINA DOVONIN   . . . .
6. CONSTANCE FINERATION   . . . .
7. NETTA FOCITUS   . . . .
8. FREDA ANNE FREESH   . . . .
9. ELIZABET FROUDE   . . . .
10. NORMAN IRONOID   . . . .
11. MICHAEL KUNKEIENSTEIN   . . . .
12. QUENTIN LARCETTI   . . . .
13. DIANA MITTELCLOZE   . . . .
14. TED MUNINI   . . . .
15. SIMON PHRYGYMINON   . . . .
16. JIM PYTHON-PURSEY   . . . .
17. CHARLES SAMPUSSISKI   . . . .
18. ANNA SEATON-RUTTER   . . . .
19. EMMA SQUIRES   . . . .
20. HANQUE TRUTT   . . . .

[Solutions on page 230]

From my early youth I had been interested in the structure of words. Reversals like 'deliver' and 'reviled' appealed to me, until I discovered palindromes – the perfect reflections that became a passion. This piece was written in 1991.

WORD-ROW REVIVER

Palindromes can be traced back as far as ancient Greece; according to Brewer, their reputed inventor was Sotades, a scurrilous Greek poet of the third century BC. The word itself comes from the Greek *palindromos*, meaning 'running back again'. Since a palindrome is a word or line reading the same both ways, the most appropriate definition would be 'word-row', though this useful term does not seem to have interested the lexicographers so far.

The English language is rich in single-word palindromes. The repetition of the consonant makes them the easiest words for a child to say, hence the names for parents: 'mum' (dialect 'mam' and US 'mom'), 'dad' and 'pop', and a grandmother is 'nan'. Even earlier, a baby imbibes mother's milk from 'tit', 'pap' or 'bub'.

Extreme vowels in three-letter palindromes are also fairly common, but do not strike the ear so readily. There is a remarkable sequence with the letter 'e' – 'ere', 'eve', 'ewe', 'Exe', 'eye' – in which the sound of the vowels is entirely dependent on the middle consonant.

Words with an odd number of letters are the most frequent, since they balance nicely on the middle letter. There is an underlying significance about words like 'level' (straight in both directions) and those indicating some kind of turning movement, as in 'radar', 'rotor', 'rotator' and 'rotavator'.

Attempts have been made to coin even longer palindromic words. The best is the eleven-letter chemical formation 'detartrated' – free of tartaric acid. Finnish goes one better with 'saippua-kauppias' – a soap-seller.

The perfect word-row would be a line constructed from individual palindromes, as in the mediaeval Latin example:

'*Anna tenet mappam, madidam mappam tenet Anna*'. But this does not seem possible in English.

It is, however, possible to manipulate a number of word reversals to form a palindromic line. The earliest in English appears to be one coined by John Taylor in 1606: 'Lewd did I live, & evil I did dwel' – though the ampersand is a bit of a cop-out. Napoleon did better with his comment (through his interpreter?): 'Able was I ere I saw Elba'.

A modern example is: 'No gateman sniper repins nametag on', which conjures up a picture of a shooting incident at the entrance to a factory involving a homicidal custodian wishing to conceal his identity.

When it comes to free-flowing palindromic sentences, English is undoubtedly the richest language, by virtue of its variety of sources and its flexibility. The most familiar is the remark attributed to the first man in the Garden of Eden, introducing himself to his lady (in English, naturally): 'Madam, I'm Adam'. She could have replied, pointing out that she is unmarried: 'Eve, Miss – I'm Eve'. A later biblical example is Noah's query to his helmsman: 'Was it Ararat I saw?'

In the latter part of the 19th century, word games became a popular family pastime, instigated by such experts as Edward Lear and Lewis Carroll. An American doctor named Charles Bombaugh published a collection of *Gleanings for the Curious from the Harvest Fields of Literature*, edited by Martin Gardner as *Oddities and Curiosities of Words and Literature* (Dover, 1961). It includes such ingenious palindromes as: 'Now stop, major-general, are negro jampots won?' and 'Stiff, O dairyman, in a myriad of fits'.

A fine palindromist working in the 20th century was Leigh Mercer. He is the author of this brilliant summary in 1914 of a civil engineering feat: 'A man, a plan, a canal – Panama!' Mercer may have been a schoolmaster, for his other well-known line is the academic dictum: 'Sums are not set as a test on Erasmus'.

More recently, there is this splendid effort by Peter Hilton, a British mathematician working as a code-breaker at

Bletchley Park during World War II: 'Doc, note I dissent. A fast never prevents a fatness. I diet on cod'.

But the greatest of modern palindromists is J.A. Lindon. In 1976 he composed an ingenious dialogue between Adam and Eve. Their union concluded with Adam's rapturous statement: 'Diamond-eyed no-maid!' Lindon may also have been the author of that acute observation: 'Sex at noon taxes'. On reflection (which one must always do with palindromes), one could visualise a matching piece of advice to lovers to complete the proverb: 'Six a.m. – maxis!'

Burton Bernstein, biographer of Thurber and younger brother of Leonard, grew up in a household where wordplay dominated the conversation. His major contribution to the art of the palindrome is a playlet entitled *Look, Ma, I Am Kool!*, published in his collection of casual pieces under that name (Prentice-Hall, 1977).

Some apposite phrases stay in the mind. One that should appeal to gardeners is: 'Goldenrod adorned log'. For teachers: 'Pupils slip up'. For music-lovers: 'If I had a hi-fi'. For a motorist's rear window: 'Pull up if I pull up!'

Efforts have been made to revive the palindrome as a literary form, for example by composing a poem in which every line is a palindrome. Although writing palindromic verse is incredibly time-consuming, particularly if it has to rhyme and scan, some enjoyable nonsense can be produced. Now and again some kind of meaning begins to emerge, as in this couplet:

> Sleepless evening, nine. Vessel peels,
> Sleek cats yell at alley, stack eels.

This is the opening of a long poem on which I've been working for some years, and which should be ready for publication in 1992. [See the next item.]

In his fascinating book *Language on Vacation* (Scribner's, 1965) Professor Dmitri Borgmann challenged anyone to write a palindromic poem. This effort, the ramblings of an elderly drunk in a seedy waterfront bar on the east coast of America, took 20 years to produce. It was published in John Julius Norwich's anthology, *More Christmas Crackers* (Penguin, 1992), and is believed to be the longest palindromic poem in English.

SENILE'S REVERIES I' REVERSE LINES

I

Sleepless evening, nine. Vessel peels,
Sleek cats yell at alley, stack eels.
Rabelais, send a sadness! I, ale-bar,
Rajah sahib at tab, I hash a jar.
Burton, odd nap, I sip and do not rub,
But liven as partner entraps an evil tub.
No, it's a bar, ever a bastion;
No ill imbibe, not one. Bib million,
Zillion US pints. If fist nip sun-oil, Liz,
Sit right, or free beer froth-girt is.
Red neb – a nostril – flirts on a bender,
Red net rabbi rose, so rib bartender.

II

'Netta Delia' sailed at ten;
Niagara, fall afar again.
Re-rack sack, can snack, cask-carer;
A rare Medoc! O Demerara!
Murder noses on red rum,
Mum, it poses optimum.
To predicate, go get a cider pot,
Toll a renegade, bed a general lot
To claret. Alas, it is a lateral cot.

Warren, slip a Pilsner raw,
Ward, regale me, lager draw;
Walter, aback sir, I risk cabaret law.

III

Night, ninth gin.
Nip ale, lap in;
Malt some most lam.
Marc in I cram,
Gorge, niff of fine grog.
Gong! Get at egg-nog.
Too hot to hoot?
Too tall a toot
To order a red root.
Tosspot tops sot
To pay a pot,
Totes in a reviver – anise tot.

IV

Retsina, call a canister;
Ruffino pull upon. If fur,
Laminate pet animal.
Laid rock, lime-milk cordial,
Dude potion sees. No, I tope dud
Dubonnet forever, often. No, bud,
No Campari. Did I rap Macon?
No net's a fillip. Ill, I fasten on
Yale belt. To bag a bottle, belay
Yard aside. Repapered is a dray.
Martini redder in it ram;
Madeira ewer. I tire, wearied am.

V

'S midnight, flew. Twelfth gin dims;
Smirnoff – it's put up, stiff on rims.
Dray, pull up yard,
Draught nets tenth guard.
Set ale, drawn inward, elates
Set at serener estates.
No garden, I left it. Feline dragon,
No gal faster frets a flagon.
Dial simple hero, more help mislaid
Diaper motto by baby bottom repaid.
Bilge, be mildewed, lime be glib,
Bird imitators rot a timid rib.

VI

Barcarolle, clever revel. Cell or a crab?
Bar delay alerts a wastrel; a Yale drab
Tastes sop, wolfs nuts. Tuns flow possets at
Tart, nor fret away a waterfront rat.
Spill a cold image, keg amid local lips,
Spirits assent. I witness Asti rips.
Strap on gateman's name-tag. No parts
Straddle if I'd roll. Lord, I field darts,
E'en knots erotic. I to rest on knee;
Emotion's sensuousness, No. 1 to me.
Pacer in mutual autumn, I recap
Pals as reviled, so red-eyed Eros delivers a slap.

Although Jean Paul Getty, the billionaire philanthropist [1892–1976], entertained lavishly at Sutton Place, his Tudor manor house in Surrey, legend has it that he installed a payphone for the use of his guests. Could it be that his personal lifestyle was sometimes frugal? This verse explores one possibility.

FOR THE FALLEN

At table, J. Paul Getty was
A man of modest taste;
He dined on simple food because
He hated any waste.

He liked to have his chef prepare
A burger in a bun,
Replete with lots of gooey fare
That tends to overrun.

He wore a kind of overall
To mop up all the mess,
Which, whimsically, he would call
The 'Getty's burger dress'.

Tom Swifties involve adverbial puns. The name is thought to derive from a character called Tom Swift in some 1920s books by Edward Stratemeyer who delivered sentences of this kind. More recently verbs have also been used to make puns. These were written in 1997/98.

TOM SWIFTIES

'Goldarn it,' myrrhmured Frank, incensed.

'Must you play records at midnight?' she said disconsolately.

'Pass me the coke!' he snorted.

'I'm determined to learn the guitar,' he said pluckily.

'Slip me a file,' the convict rasped.

'We shouldn't blame our ancestors,' he said forbearingly.

'How did you know my mother was German?' she muttered.

'My hands are numb with cold,' she cried unfeelingly.

'I'm afraid I can't wait,' he ejaculated.

'Beer's not what it was,' he complained bitterly.

'Dammit, I've scraped my shin!' he barked.

'Now I've got you!' he shouted apprehensively.

'Don't move while I'm taking your photograph,' she snapped.

'I really miss Saigon,' said the Vietnam veteran showily.

'I know who the next Pope will be,' he pontificated.

'I'm not leaving you a cent,' said his father unwillingly.

'I've got my ropes tangled,' snarled the deckhand.

'I can't find their addresses,' she said listlessly.

'Now we're divorced I want half your property,' she exclaimed.

'What's that horrible smell?' said his mother sniffily.

'I feel I'm going to die,' he croaked.

'You're fired!' said his boss dismissively.

'This parmesan is too tough,' she grated.

'Put down that gun!' said the sheriff disarmingly.

'I've put some food in your bag,' she said provisionally.

In 1951 F.S. Pearson produced a book called *Fractured French* illustrating humorous literal translations of French phrases, e.g. 'lawn-mower' for '*coup de grâce*' and 'cat-flap' for '*entrechat*'. This is a contribution to his marvellous idea.

FRENCH REFRACTURED

L'Âge d'Or	Big entrance
Aix-les-Bains	Pains of gay women
Apéritif	A set of dentures
Beau geste	A good joke
Belle de nuit	Alarm clock
Cache-sexe	Prostitute
Ça m'est égal	That's my eagle
C'est à dire	She's a dear
Chef d'oeuvre	Cook at work
Cordon bleu	Ring of police
Cordon sanitaire	Tampon
Coup de main	Major water leak
Diseuse ou midinette	10 to 12 p.m.
En avant	In a van
En dehors	On horseback
En famille	Pregnant
En fête	On foot
Faute de mieux	It's my fault
Femme fatale	Your wife's been killed
Homme d'affaires	Philanderer
Hors de concours	Racehorse
Hors d'oeuvre	Workhorse
Jolie laide	Girl who likes sex
Pièce de résistance	Girl who says no
Tour de force	Policemen's outing
Tout à coup	Wembley ticket-seller
Wagon-lit	Your car's on fire

TUTTI VERDI

To mark the centenary of Giuseppe Verdi's death in January 2001, the Royal Opera House put on a special show in which extracts from all 28 of his operas were performed. In order to remember their names, you have to imagine the great composer creating a very different and more modern piece of music:

G.V. Crafts Fast Bold Jangled Mambo

G iovanna d'Arco
V êpres Siciliennes, Les

C orsaro, Il
R igoletto
A ida
F orza del Destino, La
T raviata, La
S tiffelio

F alstaff
A roldo
S imon Boccanegra
T rovatore, Il

B attaglia di Legnano, La
O tello
L uisa Miller
D ue Foscari, I

J erusalem
A ttila
N abucco
G iorno di Regno, Un
L ombardi, I
E rnani
D on Carlos

M acbeth
A lzira
M asnadieri, I
B allo in Maschera, Un
O berto

The transposition of initial letters or sounds in two words is popularly known as a 'spoonerism', after the Rev. W.A. Spooner (1844–1930), Warden of New College, Oxford, allegedly a regular perpetrator. 'The Lord is a shoving leopard' is a famous example. Some suggested additions are given here.

DR SPOONER RIDES AGAIN

Music has Brahms to soothe a savage chest.

You need a burly chassis to belt out that song.

Matron took her exam in the knowledge of cursing.

The thief cut his hand on a blazer raid.

Her head struck the bath with a thickening sud.

I had to leave the room hurriedly, being shaken taut.

Trying to save time, the driver found a court shut.

A good hotel shouldn't allow rock coaches in.

Tom goes out more now that he has a flat cap.

It's better to avoid a road that's full of hot poles.

At a formal dance the bitter jug would be banned.

My postman's pleased with the better locks I've had fitted.

Evading the defenders, he made a great Dutch town.

I'd like these shoes to be holed and sealed.

The party was quiet until two crate gashers arrived.

It's not a fair election if you keep moving the poll ghosts.

My son likes hot dogs and not poodles.

The MFH disapproved of the ladies' hiding rabbits.

Only the keenest ecologists sign up to preen geese.

You don't need a hedge slammer to crack a nut.

Having paid for the son he dangled in the water.

Spain plotting in Greece is against the law.

It's difficult to get a drink in a crowded brush car.

Deep shipping is essential for healthy flocks.

For her party, Mrs Thatcher has been reduced to a banned hag.

With signed height, that bus should not have struck the bridge.

I'm going to a performance of *Madam Flutter-by*.

Britten's favourite was *The Stern of the Crew*.

Dickens made a pile from *The Sale of Two Titties*.

Kate is humbled in *The Shaming of the True*.

The Salad of the Bad Café is indigestible.

Bizet travelled far with *The Fare Paid of Mirth*.

Macaulay shone in *The Rays of Ancient Loam*.

Dr Spooner sometimes varied this by transposing the vowel sounds instead of the initial letters, as when he announced a hymn as 'Kinquering Kongs their titles take'. One might then say:

A Chinese restaurant needs plenty of chip stocks.

Another possible variation would be the transposition of syllables, as in:

The comic sang 'I took my part to a harpy'.

All children love *The Will in the Windows*.

Morgan – a Suitable Treat for Casement.

Many writers have formulated sententious views that have passed into the language in the same way as proverbs. Here are a few thoughts on contemporary life, laid down in 1998.

MODERN APHORISMS

The first luggage on the airport carousel is never collected.

The person sneezing on a bus or train is the one without a handkerchief.

A water-butt is full when it's raining and you don't need it, but empty in dry weather when you actually do.

The latecomer in the theatre invariably has a seat in the middle of the row.

When you're waiting for a bus, the one on your route is always going in the opposite direction.

Marriage is a life sentence, but more and more people are getting time off for bad behaviour.

Dissidents lend disenchantment to their views.

Presence of mind often makes up for absence of matter.

What you lose on the pit you may gain on the pendulum.

A pacifist doesn't always show a passive fist.

People who make generalisations are stupid.

Perversity maketh strange bedfellows.

Archaeologists are unfortunate – they'll always find their career lies in ruins.

A gynaecologist is one who listens to the patter of tiny foetuses.

More and more Catholic priests are passing their celibate date.

He's the sort of earnest ecologist who tries to monopolise the conservation.

It's better to have irons in the pie than fingers in the fire.

Conference chairmen don't enjoy their job; they just go through the motions.

In 1939 Stalin couldn't decide whether to finish off Poland or polish off Finland.

On her better days she looked as if she'd been dragged through a hedge forwards.

It's no good a writer having one foot poised on a paradox if the other is planted on a platitude.

Some Cubans are getting sick of their leader – it's known as Castroenteritis.

Politicians seeking election may count on the density of the population.

Health statisticians analyse patients broken down by age and sex.

Share-cropper: a heavy fall suffered by an investor in a declining stock market.

If there's one thing I can't stand it's intolerance!

CLOSING THE VOWELS

Writing in his *Essay on Criticism* of people who go to church just for the music, Pope said of the hymns:

> These equal syllables alone require,
> Tho' oft the ear the open vowels tire.

But would it be less tiring to the ear if the vowels were closed – for example, all of them confined to a single word?

Five words – all adjectives – in the English language contain the five vowels in alphabetical order: *abstemious, abstentious, arsenious, caesious* and *facetious.* Many other words use them all – without repetition – in various ways, their length varying from seven letters upwards.

The shortest and strangest one has five consecutive vowels: *miaoued.* This is almost equalled by the giant redwood tree, *sequoia,* with *eulogia* and *moineau* (small bastion) not far behind (we haven't yet adopted the French word *oiseau*).

Then there are several eight-letter words such as *dialogue, douanier, edacious* (gluttonous), *equation, euphobia* (fear of good news), *euphoria, jalousie* (shutter), *poulaine* (pointed shoe-toe) and *thiourea* (sulphurous carbamide).

Obviously the opportunities increase as you reach nine letters. Here are orderly definitions of some common nine-letter words containing the five essentials. Can you work them out?

1. Arsenals	11. Instruction	21. Socialist
2. Put for sale	12. Rivalry	22. Wicked
3. Ear inspector	13. Ambiguous	23. Harem slave
4. Sanction	14. Plant	24. Bone vaults
5. Car theft	15. Sweating	25. Beat a yacht
6. Examinations	16. Pet	26. Disease
7. Oven regulator	17. Leaf production	27. Tasty dishes
8. Conduct	18. Domestic	28. Determined
9. Warned	19. Immunise	29. Truthful
10. Liqueur	20. Prison	30. Troublesome

[Solutions on page 231]

In June 1973, when acting British Consul-General at Houston, I carried out two official engagements in Odessa, a small Texas oil town which boasted not only a Presidential Museum but also a perfect replica of Shakespeare's Globe Theatre complete with roof, carpets and air-conditioning. This provided the occasion for some congenial comments on our close relations.

BRITISH TIES WITH TEXAS

Thank you for inviting me to Odessa to open this fascinating exhibition on 'The British Ties of American Presidents', and the new Shakespeare season at your magnificent theatre, the Globe of the Great South-west. Perhaps one day London will have a similar tribute to Shakespeare's genius.

An Englishman often finds it embarrassing to be reminded of his country's colonial past. This is particularly true in the United States. Every November you have your Thanksgiving and in two weeks' time it will be the Fourth of July. One celebrated the arrival of a group of people who had turned their backs on their native country, and the other the cutting of the constitutional links still connecting their descendants with Britain. This history has perhaps created what the psychiatrists call a love-hate relationship between our two countries. The exhibition we see here today illustrates that the love which springs from a common heritage has proved stronger than hate.

Let us remember that the Pilgrim Fathers went to America because they wanted freedom of worship on British soil. Sailing from Plymouth in the *Mayflower*, 352 years ago, they made landfall on the coast of Massachusetts and signed the Mayflower Compact, which has been aptly called the Foundation Stone of American Liberty. That winter more than half of the 102 settlers died of cold, hunger and scurvy. But the next summer the survivors raised good crops, and their resolution never faltered. We have a lot to learn from those early pioneers.

As some of you may know, I have made a study of the

structure of words, and I find the word 'Mayflower' to be very interesting. At first sight it is simply the hawthorn. But let us turn the word backwards. We get three components: 're', a Latinism meaning regarding or about; 'wolf', meaning to eat greedily; and 'yam', an American word for the sweet potato. So we may say that, in retrospect, the Pilgrims were 'about to eat a sweet potato'. I think you will agree that, whichever way you look at it, the word 'Mayflower' is fraught with significance.

The Pilgrim Fathers spoke the language of Shakespeare, who died four years before their epic voyage, and whose memory is being splendidly honoured today by the citizens of Odessa. I understand that the language of Shakespeare's England can still be heard today in parts of rural America. I find this a comforting thought in a world that often seems to equate change with improvement. How could anybody improve on the immortal language of the Bard?

I did not realise before I came to Odessa that the first seven American Presidents were born British subjects. Out of 37 Presidents, only two appear to have been of other than British stock. If statistics are anything to go by, the next President should be of Welsh descent and his surname will contain four letters. I will leave you to check the records to see whether anyone fits this description.

When I recently visited the Alamo in San Antonio, I studied the memorial plaque to the men who fought so heroically there in 1836. It was gratifying to note that all the names were English, Welsh, Scottish or Irish. And when Texas became an independent republic Britain was the first country to open a consulate at Houston.

There have been great changes in the fortunes of our two nations and peoples in the 200 years since American Independence. Even here in Texas, Britain has experienced changes. Eighty years ago a quarter of the 64 million acres of north-west Texas were owned or financially controlled by Britain. This – regrettably or not – is no longer so. But since we fought each other two centuries ago, we have usually found ourselves on the same side. We are more likely in future to fight together than to fight each other. Our enemies are common enemies – and this produces alliances in different fields. In international affairs our partnership at times of crisis has helped to influence the shape of the world.

I'm going to close my remarks with a quotation from President Kennedy's inaugural address: 'To those old allies whose cultural and spiritual origins we share, we pledge the loyalty of faithful friends'.

[The next President was Gerald Ford!]

THE CRACKER BARREL

Where in London could one buy royal shellfish?
— King's Crustacean.

Why couldn't the train-driver's wife hang out her washing?
— Because of leaves on the line.

What famous person might you find on the deep sea bed?
— The prints of whales.

What did Italian generals lack in World War Two?
— Victory Manual.

What do some women have and others strive for?
— Sexy quality.

What dish is served at an American literary award dinner?
— Pullet Surprise.

What flight between Israel and England would be a bit OTT?
— Haifa-Luton.

How do you measure the weight of a stranded whale?
— Take it to a whale-weigh station.

What do you call the cleavage of a woman with two implants?
— Silicone Valley.

What would you expect a big Oxford Street store to do?
— Sell fridges.

Where did bomber pilots pick up their orders in a 1945 film?
— Briefing counter.

Where would you go to check a pie's weight?
— Somewhere over the rainbow.

What do you call a woman with several husbands?
— Polly Andrews.

How did Barbara Windsor describe her warm-hearted boyfriend?
— 'E's tender.

What are the funny scars on an Argentine cowboy's face called?
— Gaucho marks.

What is the name for a group of birds' nests in the Andes?
— A condorminium.

FOLLOWING THE FAITH

The people of a small village in Israel were mourning the death of their much-revered rabbi. The elders met to consider how best to honour his memory, and it was agreed that a tree should be planted as a permanent tribute.

After some discussion the men of the village decided that the most appropriate tree would be Eucalyptus.

****

A group of Taoist monks ran a banana plantation on the banks of a river. They sent their produce to market in the nearest town on a small boat, which would bring back essential supplies on the return journey. Because it travelled in both directions it was known as the 'Tao banana boat'.

****

An American touring Scotland visited a non-conformist church and met some of the congregation. He asked why the followers were known as the 'Wee Frees', and was told: 'Because there's no heating in the church'.

****

A Vatican report in March 2001 deplored the fact that an increasing number of Catholic priests, in Africa and elsewhere, were forcing nuns to be their sexual partners, and that some had produced children. It appears that these priests were taking their role as Fathers too literally.

****

Anglican clergymen are attractive to some of their female parishioners who are looking for a vicarious thrill.

ARTY-CRAFTY

A wealthy lady went into an art gallery and said to the manager: 'I just love that wall-painting your artist did for me last month, and I'd like to order another one. Do you think he could manage that for me?'

'I'm sorry, madam', the manager replied, 'you'll have to go to the Extra-Mural Department'.

****

Two art-loving Scotsmen on a walking tour in southern France were debating the best route to reach their next objective. The taller one wanted to go over the mountain range, while the shorter preferred to work his way through the river valley. As they could not agree, the little one declared:

'You take the high trek and I'll take the low trek, and I'll be in Toulouse before you'.

****

During an exhibition of contemporary artists in a Mayfair gallery a small fire broke out, threatening one of the paintings on display. It was quickly extinguished by a member of the staff, whom the owner congratulated for having saved his Bacon.

****

'I always like to see my granddaughter on her birthday, and I usually give her toys of soft material'.

'Ah, I see you like to make your presents felt'.

MUSICAL MOMENTS

An overweight tenor was appearing in a small opera house. As he made his entrance at the rehearsal the boards gave way beneath him and he went in up to his knees. An anxious singer asked whether he was all right. The producer shrugged and said: 'Don't worry – it's just a stage he's going through'.

****

A musical comedy star, having retired to a country estate, was very keen on placing statuary at strategic points. She bought an attractive bust of a composer and ordered a suitable plinth for it. The dealer, however, was unable to supply one from stock, and she had to wait for it to be delivered. But she was philosophical about the delay, saying: 'Some day my plinth will come'.

****

'My daughter's training to be an opera singer and doing very well. Now she's going to Rome to enlarge her repertoire'.
  'Why couldn't she have the operation done in London?'

****

A Cockney stripper discovered that she had something in common with Bach – an 'air on 'er G-string.

****

The conductor, taking a singer through the opera score, said: 'There's a long pause here – you could count up to ten'.
  'No problem – I'm a counter-tenor'.

****

'Did you ever propose to that girl Carmen?'
'Yes, but she said she was too Bizet to Mérimée.'

In March 1841 William Fox Talbot, the British pioneer of photography, went to Paris to show the French Academy of Sciences his photograph of the cloisters at Lacock Abbey, with the figure of a man, taken in exactly one minute.

This made a great impression on the audience, except for the President of the Academy, who was heard to murmur: '*C'est magnifique, mais ce n'est pas Daguerre*'.

****

When Peter the Great wanted an outlet on the Baltic for his navy in 1703 he had a low and swampy site drained to found the port of St Petersburg. This operation was carried out over several years by a huge number of labourers gathered from all over the province.

As a court official explained to the British Ambassador: 'We solved the labour problem by netting the serf'.

****

During the American Civil War a New York surgeon, Dr Ephraim Wilkins, devised a 'home surgery' kit for the use of soldiers with minor wounds that were not serious enough to need treatment in the overcrowded military hospitals. It was based on a simple method of stitching wounds, with a range of needles from which the soldier could select the one most appropriate for his own injury. This system was known as 'Suture-self'.

****

In June 1381 a terrified Duke of Kent burst into King Richard II's apartment and cried: 'Sire, we have a report that the peasants are revolting!' 'I know', replied the 14-year-old monarch. 'They're dirty and smelly, and I can't stand the sight of them!'

LEGAL LORE

A couple who had been married for eight years had begun to have violent quarrels. Things came to a head at their son's sixth birthday party, when the wife emptied a dish of trifle over the husband's head, and he retaliated by tipping a bowl of custard over her.

They agreed to a divorce, the main question being who should keep their son. Both parties presented their case in court, with vivid descriptions of the acts of violence. The judge listened carefully and then gave his verdict.

'I accept that the husband became a trifle upset, but that is no great matter. On the other hand, the wife has already got custardy, and I think it right that the boy should remain with her'.

****

Barrister: 'Can you think of any reason why the accused attacked you?'
Witness: 'None. All I did was to call him a deft wit'.

****

In the struggle against the gangs in the 1930s the FBI Director, J. Edgar Hoover, found it difficult to secure convictions because many people were scared to give evidence for fear of intimidation or reprisals from the Mob.

Eventually members of a strict religious sect came forward and volunteered to speak up for truth and justice. They were appropriately known as 'J.E. Hoover's Witnesses'.

****

A girl who had for years been sexually abused by her father finally got rid of him by putting bug-killer in his soup. The coroner brought in a verdict of 'Incesticide'.

BROLLY BINS AND THE GNOME TOUR

In his remarkable book on the English language, *Mother Tongue* (Penguin, 1991), Bill Bryson starts his chapter on Wordplay as follows:

> Six days a week an Englishman named Roy Dean sits down and does in a matter of minutes something that many of us cannot do at all: he completes the crossword puzzle in *The Times*. Dean is the, well, the dean of the British crossword. In 1970, under test conditions, he solved a *Times* crossword in just 3 minutes and 45 seconds, a feat so phenomenal that it has stood unchallenged for twenty years.

In 1997 BBC Radio 4 invited Bill to present a series of half-hour programmes based on *Mother Tongue*. He got in touch and arranged to interview me about crosswords and other forms of wordplay. So it came about that one afternoon in October 1997 he arrived with his producer to record our conversation.

Bill and I were miked up to the tape recorder and off we went. Without preamble he asked me to produce an anagram of his name. After considering this for a moment I pointed out the problem that there were only two vowels to play with, and too many Bs and Ls. The best I could come up with was 'Brolly Bins'. I explained that these were where the British kept their umbrellas.

'Right', said Bill, 'and now an anagram for Mother Tongue.'

'That's much easier because we have two Es – what about "The Gnome Tour"?'

Bill then introduced the programme: 'This is Brolly Bins presenting The Gnome Tour'.

During the conversation my ginger-and-white fluffy cat, Mrs Mouse, climbed on Bill's lap and got caught up in the wires. There was a plaintive mew, and I said: 'Oh, that's Mrs Mouse'.

All this was recorded, of course, and the producer was so amused that he left it in the programme, which was broadcast on 3 January 1998 and made Mrs Mouse a famous feline.

Writers of 'Letters to the Editor' know that their best efforts do not get published. Here are some examples of mine that did slip through the editorial net.

LETTERS TO THE PRESS

'So the Halifax pickets were fooled by laxative chocolate (Guardian Diary, January 24). Another case of aperients being deceptive?'

The Guardian, 30 January 1979

'It is customary to give hurricanes a name. Since we have reached the letter "E", and last Friday's storm caught us unprepared, I suggest it should be christened "Ethelred".'

The Times, 21 October 1987

'I believe that the English language is flexible enough to accommodate new words to describe new developments. In the field of economics, I suggest:
Frauditor, n., one who investigates financial irregularities.
Stockbroken, adj., ruined by rash market speculation.'

The Times, 17 May 1988

['Frauditor' was immediately taken up by the media, but has not yet appeared in any of the major English dictionaries.]

'It is noticeable in television crime series that the police so seldom bother to lock their cars when they get out. Even Inspector Morse sets an occasionally bad example. He should realise, as a regular solver of anagrams in *The Times* crossword, that he may be turning persons to crime.'

The Times, 2 January 1996

'Gill conjures up a picture of twin towns with little in common. But it should be possible to match partners more closely. In ports, for example, Hull could be twinned with Kiel, and Bristol with Brest.'

Sunday Times, 23 February 1997

'A comment on the recent England international:

> A confident coach called Glenn Hoddle
> Thought that beating the Swedes was a doddle,
> But a fast-moving team
> Put an end to his dream;
> He'll have no regrets, but his squad'll.'

The Times, 14 September 1998

'In the C&G Final (report, 3 September), was it not inevitable that poor Boswell (Leicestershire) should toil in the shadow of mighty Johnson (Somerset)?'

The Times, 7 September 2001

PARODIES

In the late 1930s I became hooked on the 'Just William' stories by Richmal Crompton. The books were printed in Watford and given to me by relatives who worked in the plant. They inspired the following parody written in 1942. At that time I wondered where William's village of Hadley was; it was not until I moved to Bromley in 1970 that I discovered the author had been a teacher in the local girls' High School. When she retired from teaching in 1924 she had a spacious house called 'The Glebe' built in Oakley Road, off Bromley Common, which now bears a blue plaque in her honour. Oakley Road leads to Hayes, so it is not impossible that Hadley had its origins in a composite of Hayes and Bromley.

WILLIAM THE WAR-WINNER

William and the Outlaws were slowly trudging down the dusty road that ran through their village to Hadley. It was the summer holiday and they were bored. William disconsolately sucked a bullseye, Ginger was kicking a rusty can along the road, Henry tried in vain to juggle with two round pebbles, and Douglas was gloomily throwing stones at trees, missing his target every time. Jumble was playfully leaping in and out of a ditch and scratching the earth up in search of rats.

William at length munched the last of his bullseye and turned to the Outlaws. Ginger kicked his can into the ditch, and Henry threw away his pebbles in disgust. Douglas hurled one last stone (hitting a cow in a field and sending it lumbering away bellowing), and joined the others. Jumble reluctantly left the ditch and trotted at William's heels.

William was the first to speak. 'Wot can we do that we haven't done before?' he said at last. 'We've made a seaside an' had a show thing, and bin Mare and Corperayshun, an' anyway I'm tired o' Red Injuns.'

'H'm,' said Douglas scornfully, 'an' a fine lot o' profit we got outa that seaside an' that ole show. Everythin' we do seems to go wrong.'

'I vote we do somethin' intrestin' for a change,' said Henry, ''stead o' playin' the same ole games all the time.'

'Yes,' Ginger put in eagerly, ''s about time we did somethin' new.'

'Well,' said William, 'have you got any serjestyuns?'

'Coo, yes,' Douglas exclaimed. 'I remember now I come to think of it! I heard some men sayin' they wanted some mettul stuff to build airerplanes. Ally-ally somethin' it's called.'

'I know what it is,' said Henry. 'It's allyminum! I heard my mother sayin' somethin' about it to father yesterdy. It's in pots and pans an' suchlike, an' the Gov'ment are 'pealing for people to collect it.'

'I know,' said William, voicing the thoughts of all four. 'Let's get some of this allyminum stuff an' take it to these men. We could help to win the war.'

'Yes, let's,' echoed the Outlaws simultaneously.

'But how're we gonna get it?' said Henry thoughtfully. 'My mother said she couldn't afford to give any of her utensulls away 'cos she wouldn't have enough to cook with.'

'Yes, an' I bet my parents wouldn't let me have any, either. They're orfully mean. All grown-ups are,' Douglas said bitterly.

'No, I don't s'pose they would,' agreed William. 'Then we'll have to think of some plan to get 'em,' he added vaguely.

'Well, think of one then,' said Ginger. 'You're s'posed to be good at plans.'

'Yes, think of a plan,' Henry and Douglas cried together.

'Orlrite, then, I will,' said William hastily. 'You jus' wait a minnit an' see.'

William eyed the ground desperately for a few minutes, and at length looked up, a gleam in his eye.

'Well?' chorused the Outlaws.

'I gotter plan,' said William importantly, 'an' a jolly good plan an' all! I bet not many people could've thought of a plan as quick as that.'

'Go on,' Ginger exclaimed, 'tell us yore plan.'

'Orlrite, orlrite,' said William, and then seeing that the Outlaws had no wish to hear about his mental prowess, he unfolded his plan to them.

His idea was received with joyous acclamation by the others, and they agreed to adopt it and carry it out. Douglas was as usual a trifle pessimistic. 'Wot if our parents don't 'preshiate what we've done?' he queried. 'They never seem to 'preshiate what we do.'

'Oh, they will,' said William with his usual optimism, 'when they unnerstand it's 'cos of the Gov'ment an' the war.'

At this Douglas' fears were allayed, and the Outlaws separated for their homes in a great state of anticipation.

After their mid-day meal (the Outlaws always ate a large meal in case it should be their last) four mothers were informed earnestly by their sons that a cow now inhabited their respective back gardens. At this news three of them went out to inspect this phenomenon, but after a diligent search (which revealed no cow) each frowningly returned to her house to find her son departed, she knew not whither. The three mothers shrugged their shoulders and went on with their work in the kitchen, as did the fourth.

The Outlaws met on the village street and proceeded towards Hadley. William surveyed his men with pride and approval. Ginger wore on his head two saucepans, the lids of which he continually clashed together. Henry had a selection of knives, forks and spoons, and also carried an old dustbin lid which he kept on beating with a large spoon, while William himself had a kettle and several tins, which he claimed to be made of allyminum.

Poor Douglas explained that he had been unable to convince his mother as to the presence of a cow in the back garden. He said he had also tried to persuade her to go and answer the telephone, but with equal firmness she replied that it had not rung.

'It would've been jus' the same if it *had* rung,' he complained bitterly. 'I bet there's some lor about folks who don't answer their telephones. She could've bin sent to prison,' he added vengefully.

'Never mind,' said William. 'We've got enuff orlreddy, an' we don't want to take too much.'

At that moment they happened to be passing a knife-grinder's handcart, the owner of which was wistfully eyeing the Huntsman's Arms which stood opposite. When he caught sight of the Outlaws he looked at William distastefully, and cried out: 'Hey, you young 'erbs, cum over 'ere.'

The Outlaws came towards him suspiciously.

'Well,' said William, 'what've we done wrong?'

'Lots of fings, by the looks of yer,' said the knife-grinder, chuckling at his joke. 'Orlright, I'm not goin' to bite yer. I wants yer to look after me barrer while I pops inter the pub over there an' 'as a glass o' lemmernade. I'll give yer tuppence if everyfink's OK when I gets back, but not before.'

'Orlright,' said William, 'we'll look after yore ole barrer. But don't forget the tuppence.'

His words fell on empty air, however, for the grinder was already in the inn and ordering his 'lemmernade'.

The Outlaws examined the machinery for a minute or two to see now it worked. Then Henry produced a knife and said: 'Let's sharpen this knife. Shorely he won't mind an' we won't hurt his ole barrer.'

'Yes, let's,' chorussed the others.

'Bags me first,' William got in quickly.

'Coo, no,' objected Henry. ''S my knife, isn't it?'

'Fight you for it,' cried William, and Henry agreed.

A short and sharp battle ensued. William emerged victorious if rather battered, and seizing the knife began to work the handle that turned the grindstone, slowly at first but then more vigorously. When he looked at the knife, however, he found to his consternation that the blade had almost disappeared. All that was left of it was in the form of a small heap of powdered metal on the ground.

William stared from the handle in his hand to the grey heap under the barrow. Then a look of exultance spread over his grimy features, and he said: 'Gimme another one, quick.'

'No,' said Henry stoutly, 'it's my turn.'

50

'Orlrite,' William agreed reluctantly. 'Orl of you have yore turn quick, an' then I c'n have another go.'

Henry had his go, obviously enjoying it immensely. Then he handed a knife to Ginger, who eagerly transformed the blade into powder in double-quick time. Douglas then swiftly added his blade to the fast-growing heap of powder. This threatened to attain huge dimensions, and most assuredly would have done so if a little girl had not trotted up with a handful of knives and demanded to ''ave 'em sharped up in a jiffy or her mum would know the reason why'.

William took a knife from the bundle and put it under the demolition process. In a minute the blade had joined the heap. When Ginger had done the same to another knife the little girl opened her mouth and began to cry loudly. Then she ran back to her home and howled to her mother: 'Mum, mum, there's a narsty boy at the barrer and 'e's bin an' gorn an' grinded orl the knives awa-a-a-ay.'

On hearing this alarming news, a grim and determined woman in a dirty apron approached the grinder's barrow just as the flushed man staggered out of the Huntsman's Arms, having thoroughly enjoyed more than one glass of 'lemmernade'.

She stamped up to the inebriated grinder, who muttered thickly: 'Woshermatter?'

'Where's that boy o' yourn,' demanded the angry woman. 'Look wot 'e's gorn an' done to me knives! Ruined 'em, 'e 'as. Where's the young varmint, eh?'

The grinder stupidly eyed the knife handles and the heap of powder on the ground. At length he grasped the situation, and gave a bellow of rage.

'Yus, where is 'e?' he cried, losing forth a stream of invective at which even the woman blanched.

But William and the Outlaws had set off at the approach of the woman, and they were already out of sight round the corner on their way to Hadley.

The grinder gave one last volley of abuse, and turned to examine the machinery on his cart in case it had been damaged. Fortunately it was not, so he shook his fist in the direction of the departed Outlaws and muttered something about 'skinnin' the little devils if 'e ever cort 'em'.

Meanwhile the Outlaws were walking gaily along the road, discoursing on the subject of winning the war.

Henry, the most learned, was just giving his views on how long the war would last when a lorry came up and drew to a stop alongside. The driver asked Henry if he was on the right road to Hadley, and Henry said he was. The driver thanked him, and prepared to pull away. William looked at the Outlaws and signalled them to climb on the back of the lorry. Then he himself ran to the cab and called to the driver.

'You did say Hadley, didn't you?' he asked.

'Yes, I did,' the driver replied.

'Oh, I thort you did,' said William, disappearing behind the lorry.

The driver scratched his head in puzzlement, unaware that he now had a load of stowaways, and drove off.

William looked proudly at the Outlaws. 'Now we'll get to Hadley much quicker,' he exclaimed.

The Outlaws were by now exploring the interior of the lorry. Suddenly Henry found two sacks. He looked inside and gave a cry of joy. 'Look at this – it's orl allyminum!'

They hauled out the sacks and examined the contents. Sure enough, the sacks contained kettles and shiny saucepans, and other merchandise of that metal. They each helped themselves to a few, depositing their own worn goods in exchange. Then the driver pulled up in Hadley High Street to deliver to the big store what he assumed to be new kitchenware.

The Outlaws jumped down and sped off in the direction of the Market Square, where the precious aluminium was being collected. Here they handed in their haul, to the collector's delight, and were thanked profusely for their pains. Then they returned slowly back through Hadley, halting every now and then to look in a shop window.

Outside one shop Douglas found half-a crown caught in a crack in the pavement. This was riches indeed. Most of the Outlaws wanted to spend it all at once, but the cautious

Douglas was all for keeping some by for another time. As it was his find, they agreed to reserve a shilling 'for a rainy day', as Douglas put it.

Threepence went to buy a package of acid drops, and the remaining money bought a large bag of sickly-looking cream puffs at a pastry shop. The Outlaws took the puffs outside and fell to eating them with relish, much to the consternation of an elderly woman who appeared alarmed at the fast disappearance of the pastries. This good lady blinked at the Outlaws for a moment, then walked away shaking her head.

Having demolished the puffs, the Outlaws departed homewards munching the acid drops. On their way home they happened to pass an apple orchard belonging to one of their enemies, Farmer Roberts. As their supplies of acid drops were exhausted they decided to lay in a stock of apples. Henry therefore scaled the wall of the orchard and crept forward to reconnoitre. He returned with the good news that there was no one about and the trees were loaded with apples.

The Outlaws promptly clambered over the wall and set about stripping the nearest tree. Each had filled his pockets when a gruff voice, mingled with the shrill yapping of a dog, bellowed: 'Coom on 'ere, yer young rascals. Cort yer red'anded, ain't Oi.'

At this the Outlaws turned tail and fled towards the wall and the safety that lay beyond it, hotly pursued by the farmer and his dog. Ginger took the wall in his stride, Henry followed him, then William, and Douglas was halfway over when a heavy stick came down with a thwack on his leg. Poor Douglas toppled over the wall and lay on the ground groaning, assuring the Outlaws that his leg was broken.

'That'll larn yer to keep aht o' me orchard, yer little imps,' laughed the farmer triumphantly.

The Outlaws helped Douglas to his feet, and he limped after them. They walked along in comparative silence, munching their apples. Douglas was still muttering about his bad luck, but otherwise they were pleased with their day's work. They passed through their village without meeting the knife-grinder and his barrow, and separated for their homes, after deciding to meet in the Old Barn the following day to consider any unforeseen consequences.

It was a sorry band of Outlaws who met in the Old Barn the next morning.

'I gotta good hidin' an' had to go to bed without any supper,' said William.

'I bet I gotta worse hidin' than you did,' claimed Ginger. 'My father nearly killed me, an' I'm still sore.'

'I don't know how they 'spect us to sleep when we're achin' orl over,' moaned Henry.

'An' Farmer Roberts came roun' to see my father in the evenin', and I got another thrashin' larst night,' groaned Douglas.

'An' they've stopped my pocket money for three months to pay for their ol' kettle,' complained William. 'That's orl the thanks we get for tryin' to help 'em win the war.'

Ginger and Henry said miserably that they had been treated similarly.

'An' they'll prob'ly take mine when yore parents tell 'em,' added Douglas mournfully. 'Grown-ups ARE mean!'

'Oh, I'm sick o' winnin' the war,' said William. 'Let's go an' play pirates in the wood.'

'Yes, let's,' said the Outlaws eagerly, and they ran into the woods shouting bloodthirsty battle cries.

A voyage to Colombo in the liner *Warwickshire* in 1958 produced mixed feelings, summed up in this version of a great song from the 1930s.

MARITIME MEMORIES

The deck that wobbles and is never stable,
The conversation at the Captain's table,
The way salt water stings –
These foolish things remind me of you.

The dinner jacket with those gravy traces,
The cummerbund that's worn instead of braces,
Black ties like knotted strings –
These foolish things remind me of you.

You steamed across the ocean blue;
Each time I think of you
I breathe the faint oily stink of you.

The stroll around the deck in tropic moonlight
The cabin door that's left ajar at midnight,
The creaking of the springs –
These foolish things remind me of you.

In the 1945 film musical, *State Fair*, the biggest hit was the Rodgers & Hammerstein ballad, 'It Might as Well be Spring'. The lyric seemed to call for an alliterative version.

THOUGHTS ON SEEING *STATE FAIR*

I'm as anxious as an adder in an ant-hill,
I'm as batty as the balm that breezes bring,
I'm as crazy as the concrete in my courtyard,
And it isn't even spring.

I'm as dotty as dalmatians in a dogpound,
I'm as errant as an elver eddying,
I'm as frantic as a ferret in a frenzy;
What has happened to the spring?

I'm as ghoulish as a gargoyle in a graveyard,
I'm as hazy as a hedgehog havering,
I'm as icy as an ibex in an igloo,
'Cos we haven't seen the spring.

I'm as jumpy as a jackal in the jungle,
I'm as kinky as the killer of a king,
I'm as loopy as a lasso on a lamp-post,
And I'm longing for the spring.

I'm as moody as a miser with his money,
I'm as nutty as a noodle in Nanking,
I'm as oval as an orange in an orchard,
Getting ready for the spring.

I'm as pungent as a polecat in a panic,
I'm as queasy as a Quaker quarrelling,
I'm as restless as a rabbit in a rainstorm,
Will we never see the spring?

I'm as sullen as a striker in a sit-down,
I'm as tortured as a traveller from Tring,
I'm as ugly as an undernourished uncle,
Praying daily for the spring.

I'm as vacant as a villa in the valley,
I'm as witless as a widgeon on the wing,
I'm excited as an extra in an X-film,
Can this really be the spring?

I'm as yellow as a yaffle in the Yukon,
I'm as zany as a zebra zigzagging,
And now I'm running out of letters,
And I've really had my fling,
But I have to say,
In an alphabetic way,
That it might as well be spring.
It might as well be spring.

An entry for a competition run by Shell-Mex & BP Ltd in 1968 for a poem in the style of Kipling to mark the future introduction of a new airline flying Concorde.

CONCORDIA AIRWAYS

Awake, ye Welsh and English men,
Ye Scots and Ulstermen, arise;
The island race is great again –
Concordia Airways rules the skies.
O God on high, be with us yet
In Britain's supersonic jet.

The shrieking turbine's thrusting powers
Shall whittle distances away –
To Singapore in seven hours,
Australia in half a day.
Let lesser breeds their pride forget
In Britain's supersonic jet.

Wider shall grow this mighty line
Till its majestic eagles range
Their pinions over palm and pine,
Unhindered by the winds of change.
O God on high, be with us yet
In Britain's supersonic jet.

Clement Attlee once recalled that in his Oxford days he wrote a poem for *Isis* beginning: 'When I am walking down the High, And meet my favourite Blue'. A literary competition in 1974 invited readers to complete the poem.

FAME

When I am walking down the High
And meet my favourite Blue,
I cannot look him in the eye,
But mumble 'How d'you do?'

He is a man of soaring fame,
While I live very flatly;
I doubt if he has heard the name
Of Clement Richard Attlee.

He is the hero of the hour,
I am a humble sheep.
And yet I feel a hidden power –
Still waters running deep.

I know that I shall one day be
As great and strong a man as he.

Wordsworth complained that a satirical quatrain by Dr Johnson was 'not interesting – does not lead to anything'. This entry to a literary competition in 1974 was an attempt to carry the great lexicographer's poem forward in dramatic style.

BRIEF ENCOUNTER

I put my hat upon my head
And walked into the Strand,
And there I met another man
Whose hat was in his hand.

His suit of black, his air of woe,
Showed him to be a mourner.
I asked him why he trembled so
And wept on the street corner.

'I am a turnip-crier,' he said,
'I loved my father dearly.
Alas, that poor old man is dead;
I grieve for him sincerely.'

'Why, sir,' said I, 'away with grief,
And be a lively fellow.
You merely need, in my belief,
An hour in a bordello.'

He had a pistol in his hat,
He aimed it at my head,
And crying: 'Get a load of that'
He pumped me full of lead.

Hilaire Belloc's Lord Finchley (*More Peers*, 1911) met his end when trying to mend the electric light instead of employing an artisan. The striking similarity of a French singer's death in 1978 prompted this tasteless verse, submitted to *Punch* and quite properly rejected.

ON THE DEATH OF A SINGER

(After Belloc)

Claude François tried to fix the bathroom light
Himself. It struck him dead, and serve him right.
It is the duty of the pop musician
To give employment to the electrician.

Leigh Hunt's Jenny was possibly about ten years old when she kissed him. This entry to a literary competition visualises her 30 years on.

JENNY AT 40

Jenny kissed me when we met
Looking rather fat and frisky;
Rancid reek of cigarette
Mingled with the fumes of whisky.
Though I'm short of female chums
(Truth to tell, I haven't any),
When the Day of Judgment comes
Spare me Jenny!

The opening scene of a dramatic play (unfinished), published in the Diplomatic Service Wives' *Bulletin* in 1984.

TIRELESS AMBASSADOR

A Dramatic Fragment of Diplomatic Life

Act I, Scene I – A diplomatic mission in Africa.
                An AMBASSADOR addresses his minions.

AMB So meet we here to make a true report
       Which shall acquaint our officers of state
       With late intelligence of dire events
       In this unruly land.

       (Enter a SECOND SECRETARY)

                    What tidings, sirrah?

SEC My lord, I come in haste from far Magamba,
       Whose dusty streets now flow with lancéd blood.
       'Tis said the ballot hath been foully rigged;
       The politicians have deceived the people,
       Who now avenge themselves. In wildest rage
       They seize their masters and dismember them
       With hissing matchets, limb from bloody limb.
       Meantime th' opposing party, hopes frustrate,
       Hath armed its thugs for battle. Shrieking hordes,
       Drunk on raw spirit, leap into the fray
       And plunge the country into hideous war.
       I fear no aid can come from the militia
       In such a pass. 'Tis each man for himself,
       And devil take the hindmost. Yesternight
       The maddened rabble took a deadly toll
       Of mammy wagons on the motor roads;
       Each highway now is choked with smoking cars
       Whose ruins reek of human flesh. In short,
       We are beleaguered.

AMB   We thank thee for thy pains.
        An MBE shall be thy just reward.
        Now set the printer to its magic work,
        And let the wingéd messages go forth
        With most immediate speed. Nothing encypher,
        But let the language speak both plain and frank,
        Telling the tale before this day be o'er;
        That sleepy clerks residing in Whitehall
        Shall know what monstrous happenings befall.

                (Exeunt omnes)

A tribute to the late Poet Laureate, submitted to a weekly competition in June 1984. Like his 'Hymn', it can be sung to the tune of 'The Church's one foundation'.

HOMAGE TO BETJEMAN

When Betjeman departed
In nineteen eighty-four
It left us heavy-hearted
To hear his voice no more.
His lyrical achievement
We all could understand,
And pangs of keen bereavement
Were felt throughout the land.

The comedy of manners
Was his essential strain;
Pretentious snobs and planners
Were mocked in tones urbane.
He did not seek to lecture,
But taught us to admire
Victorian architecture
In arch and roof and spire.

He carried his researches
From Cornwall to the Fens;
Great houses, villas, churches
All came before his lens.
And as he told the story
Of Salisbury or Wells
He summoned up the glory
Expressed in pealing bells.

He sang the muscled maiden,
The fragrant Surrey pines,
The cliffs with blossom laden,
Suburban railway lines.
And while a handsome station
Was lauded in his verse,
He showed that restoration
Could lead to something worse.

A morbid dread of dying
Disturbed his later years,
Though friends were always trying
To dissipate his fears.
May all his troubles cease now
Where waves assault the rock,
And may he rest in peace now
In far St Enodoc.

Competitors were asked to take Lovelace's famous lyric in a different, modern direction, using the same metre and rhyme-scheme. This entry was published in the *Spectator* in 1986; it also appeared as an appropriate chapter heading in Colin Dexter's last Morse novel, *The Remorseful Day* (2000).

LOVELACE BLEEDING

Don't tell me, sweet, that I'm unkind
Each time I black your eye,
Or raise a weal on your behind –
I'm just a loving guy.

I love it when you scratch and bite
And leave me feeling bruised;
Unless we fought throughout the night
I wouldn't be amused.

We both despise the gentle touch,
So cut out the pretence;
You wouldn't love it half as much
Without the violence.

Cole Porter's song in *Can-Can* inspired this 1984 comment on Mrs Thatcher's attitude towards our French partners.

MAGGIE'S LAMENT

(*Can't-Can't*)

I loathe Paris very deeply,
I loathe Paris more and more;
I loathe Paris for the rudeness of the folk there,
I loathe Paris for the Gauloises that they smoke there.
I loathe Paris for its pissoirs,
And that awful garlic stench;
I loathe Paris – why, oh why, do I loathe Paris?
Because it's full of French!

An attempt to write a parody of a great sonnet while retaining the original's rhyme-endings. Written 1991, unpublished.

WORDSWORTH REVIEWS THE SITUATION

The world is too much for me. Pretty soon,
Seeking an ending, I'll lay waste my powers.
Fiddle-de-dee! That wretched brat of ours
Has hidden my blades away. Well, that's a boon;
I'd hate to bare my bosom to the moon
When winds may still be howling. In the small hours
I'll hang uptethered, owl-like. Please, no flowers,
No organ, for the thing is out of tune
As like as not. Good Heavens! Can it be
My braces, buckled, were decreed outworn?
So fate is smiling on me pleasantly;
What glimpses then would make me less forlorn?
I'll join the motorists driving to the sea,
And steer through Brighton blowing on my horn!

The centenary of Housman's 'A Shropshire Lad' was celebrated in 1996. This affectionate tribute to him was published by my old colleague John Julius Norwich in his annual 'Christmas Cracker' and reprinted in his anthology *Still More Christmas Crackers* (Viking, 2000). It was also set to the music of Schubert's *Trout* (published by DaCapo Music Ltd in 2000).

A SHROPSHIRE LASS

In spring the hawthorn scatters
Its snow along the hedge,
And thoughts of country matters
Run strong on Wenlock Edge.

So fared I, loose and feckless,
And met a maiden fair;
She wore an amber necklace
To match her tawny hair.

Her mouth was soft and willing,
Her eyes were like the sea;
I offered her a shilling
If she would lie with me.

At that she blushed so sweetly,
And cast her fine eyes down;
Then, whispering discreetly,
Suggested half-a-crown.

This entry in the 1997 Housman Society Poetry Competition was shortlisted, and published in the anthology *Departures*. It was also read at the annual Housman Memorial Service in Ludlow Church in April 1998.

A SOMERSET LAD

Harold Gimblett (1914–78), a former Somerset and England batsman, was barred from the Long Room at Lord's in 1977 because he was not a member of the MCC. Already sick and suffering from depression, he died by his own hand in the following year.

> Harold, lad, you've hit your wicket,
> Quit a life whose pitch was flat.
> Once you topped the world of cricket,
> Wielding high the willow bat.
>
> Then your bronzed and brawny forearms
> Rippling smote the leathern sphere,
> Till the bowlers cursed their sore arms
> And the fieldsmen fled in fear.
>
> You were not the lad to linger,
> Knew your innings could not last;
> Walked before the umpire's finger
> Beckoned, smiling as you passed.
>
> Entry to the Lord's Pavilion
> Can no longer be denied;
> Now's your chance to make a million
> Batting on the other side.

A study of 'A Shropshire Lad' shows that A.E. Housman may have been a keen sportsman, if not a great performer himself. For example, football is mentioned twice, and in poem XVII he writes:

> Now in Maytime to the wicket
> Out I march with bat and pad.

What might he have thought of modern goings-on in the game?

NOT CRICKET

Cricket now with strife is riven,
Sportsmanship's gone to the bad;
Batsmen stand their ground when given
Out to catch off bat and pad.

Bowlers tend to see the stump higher
Than would give a leg before,
Loud appealing to the umpire,
Cursing that his eyesight's poor.

Keepers claim the batsman's edging
Catches to the slips array,
Then resort to angry sledging
When they cannot get their way.

Sullied is the name of cricket
While these vandals still persist;
I'm not marching to the wicket
Till the last has been dismissed.

Housman's love of cricket is also shown in this little verse.

THE SUMMER GAME

Lads, to pleasure cricket lovers,
Pull with lusty strokes to leg;
Drive the loose balls through the covers,
Guarding well their middle peg.

Working up from slow beginnings,
Faster then from hook and sweep;
Scoring with a thrustful innings
Ere they hole out in the deep.

Shelley's sonnet 'Ozymandias' was neatly brought to earth by the distinguished American scholar, Professor Morris Bishop, who transcribed the last three lines to condemn the witless modern tourists who are compelled to leave their names everywhere. This is an attempt to Anglicise his jest.

OZYMANDIAS REVISITED

I met a traveller from an antique land
Who said: Two vast and trunkless legs of stone
Stand in the desert. Near them, on the sand,
Half sunk, a shattered visage lies, whose frown,
And wrinkled lip, and sneer of cold command,
Tell that its sculptor well those passions read
Which yet survive, stamped on these lifeless things,
The hand that mocked them, and the heart that fed.
And on the pedestal these words appear:
'My name is Ozymandias, King of Kings.
Look on my works, ye Mighty, and despair!'
Cut in beside the names of Eddie Kaye,
Rebecca Russell, Rex Bowness, Ann Baer,
And Joan and Ethel Sands of Galloway.

A favourite literary competition in the weekly magazines asks you to take a well-known line of verse and add an incongruous rhyming line to achieve a bathetic effect. The first Brooke entry was published in the *Spectator* in 1984, and in *The Wit of the Spectator* (Century, 1989). The first Wordsworth entry was published in the *New Statesman* in 1974, and in *Never Rub Bottoms With a Porcupine* (Allen & Unwin, 1979). I call my entries for this game

DECOUPLETS

Blake
> And did those feet in ancient time
> Need a hot bath to cleanse the grime?

Brooke
> If I should die, think only this of me:
> 'He never made it to Gallipoli'.

> Unkempt about these hedges blows
> A filthy tramp his streaming nose.

> And in my flower-beds, I think,
> Some mongrel's droppings quietly stink.

> Breathless, we flung us on the windy hill,
> And suddenly were violently ill.

> Fish (fly-replete in depth of June)
> Cooked in my pan this afternoon.

> And oft between the boughs is seen
> A ginger tomcat with his queen.

Browning

Dauntless the slug-horn to my lips I set,
But spat it out, all slimy, foul and wet.

Grow old along with me,
In pensioned poverty.

Ah, did you once see Shelley plain,
Or was he handsome, proud and vain?

Byron

She walks in beauty like the night,
But in the daylight – what a fright!

There was a sound of revelry by night
As soccer hooligans prepared to fight.

I stood in Venice on the Bridge of Sighs;
A dead dog floated by before my eyes.

Coleridge

The shadow of the dome of pleasure
Lifted by loads of Lottery treasure.

It was a miracle of rare device,
And so it should be, at that awful price!

Donne

Go and catch a falling star
Who's had too many at the bar.

Busy old fool, unruly Sun,
Elections not by thee are won.

Hardy

This is the weather the cuckoo likes,
And leathered louts on motor-bikes.

Herrick

A sweet disorder in the dress
Can soon become an awful mess.

When as in silks my Julia goes
She has no need for nylon hose.

Gather ye rose-buds while ye may;
Their scent will drive the lice away.

Housman

When I was one-and-twenty
Of crumpet I had plenty.

Into my heart an air that kills
Reminded me to take my pills.

Loveliest of trees, the cherry now
Has corpses hanging anyhow.

Jonson

Drink to me only with thine eyes,
And never look at other guys.

Keats

A thing of beauty is a joy for ever –
And twice as interesting if she's clever.

Much have I travelled in the realms of gold,
And made enough to keep me when I'm old.

Season of mists and mellow fruitfulness,
And floods that leave the village in a mess.

When I have fears that I may cease to be
There's nothing nicer than a pot of tea.

Landor

I strove with none, for none was worth my strife,
Until I went and got myself a wife.

Marlowe

Was this the face that launched a thousand ships,
And graced the page from which I eat my chips?

Marvell

Had we but world enough and time
We'd take off to a warmer clime.

How vainly men themselves amaze
To win the pools on Saturdays.

My vegetable love shall grow
To win a prize at this year's show.

Annihilating all that's made
With one atomic cannonade.

Where the remote Bermudas ride
No inch of thigh can be espied.

Milton

When I consider how my light is spent
I put a shilling in the meter's vent.

They also serve who only stand and wait,
So mind you leave a tip beside your plate.

Of man's first disobedience, and the fruit,
I think a dozen longish books should suit.

Blest pair of Sirens, pledges of Heaven's joy,
Twin globes whereon my hands delight to toy.

Pope
> The proper study of mankind is man,
> But woman's worth some study if you can.

Scott
> The way was long, the wind was cold,
> The minstrel slipped and down he rolled.

> O what a tangled web we weave
> Of worldwide dotcom make-believe!

Shakespeare
> My mistress' eyes are nothing like the sun,
> But small and dark, like currants in a bun.

> He hath a strange infirmity from his youth;
> The doctors think it's Aids, to tell the truth.

> Shall I compare thee to a summer's day?
> No, winter's night would be an apter way.

> There's a divinity that shapes our ends,
> And drives the church to happy-clappy trends.

> Fear no more the heat o' the sun –
> The English summer has begun.

> Golden lads and girls all must
> Refrain from unprotected lust.

> If music be the food of love, play on;
> But if it's dreadful rock and roll – begone!

> To be, or not to be: that is the question;
> Would someone like to offer a suggestion?

> Now is the winter of our discontent
> Discomfiting a hapless government.

There is a tide in the affairs of men
When girl-friends fail to call them back again.

Where the bee sucks, there suck I;
He's stung my lip and made me cry!

'Tis not in mortals to command success
Without the backing of the tabloid press.

By the pricking of my thumbs
And fingers, I do simple sums.

When icicles hang by the wall,
Then bicycles stand in the hall.

Friends, Romans, countrymen, lend me your ears –
The barber's taken mine off with his shears.

When shall we three meet again?
Say, five o'clock in Drury Lane?

Once more unto the breach, dear friends, once more,
And I'll be standing here to keep the score.

I know a bank whereon the wild thyme blows;
You can't get money now – it's had to close.

Shelley
I met a traveller from an antique land
Who pressed a filthy postcard in my hand.

Music, when soft voices die,
Tortures if the sound's too high.

Tennyson
Now sleeps the crimson petal, now the white,
And I'm so bushed I'll go out like a light.

It little profits that an idle king
Should wither under Mrs Simpson's wing.

And slowly answered Arthur from the barge:
'Now, Lancelot, I'm leaving you in charge.'

'Tis better to have loved and lost
Than marry and be badly bossed.

I come from haunts of coot and hern,
And tread on them at every turn.

Wordsworth
　Bliss was it in that dawn to be alive,
　Struggling to catch the 7.45.

Earth has not anything to show more fair
Than Celia sleeping, pink and plump, and bare.

Strange fits of passion have I known
When window salesmen ring my phone.

I wandered lonely as a cloud
Of broken wind dispersed the crowd.

My heart leaps up when I behold
The profits on the shares I sold.

She dwelt among the untrodden ways,
And served cream teas on dainty trays.

She was a phantom of delight
Until the spirits made her tight.

Yeats
　When you are old and grey and full of sleep
　There won't be any need for counting sheep.

Down by the salley gardens my love and I did meet
Until her husband caught us and forced me to retreat.

Had I the heavens' embroidered cloths
I'd try to save them from the moths.

****

A variation on a popular TV theme song, written for the 1997
General Election, but not used.

LOVES LABOUR'S WON

Labour, everybody should be Labour,
It's the party of the people
To support on polling day.
Labour wants to work for all the nation,
And to repair eighteen years of decay.

Labour's so much better than the Tories,
It's the care and understanding
That distinguish us from them;
Labour's ready for the great election,
That's when our leader becomes P.M.

SPOOFS

This flight of fancy was written in the dark days of 1943 to entertain my schoolmates. They still recall it over 50 years later.

A MODERN CANDLE FACTORY

Upon occasions, in the erratic course of events of strenuous wartime, a power station is put out of action, or some similar mishap occurs to deprive the public of its invaluable electricity supply. In these circumstances, a vast section of the community is reduced to the employment of candles for the maintenance of precious lighting.

Little does the housewife know, as she unthinkingly applies match to wick to acquire the subsequent illumination, of the divers intricate processes which have been put into execution to bear fruit in that insignificant but extremely useful little article, the common candle. How few people value this humble device at its true worth, merely deeming it a makeshift upon the failure of the electric light. Truly this is an unfortunate instance of familiarity breeding contempt!

Reposing in comfortable meditation, my thoughts rambling incoherently from one subject to another, I was suddenly struck by the above-mentioned observation, and I saw the candle in an entirely different light from that to which I had previously been accustomed. Immediately I was seized with an insatiable curiosity as to the nature of the processes culminating in the production of the commonplace household candle, and I forthwith resolved to pay a tour of inspection into its origins and manufacture.

Putting my desire into effect, I obtained the necessary permission for my visit to the candle factory, and the following afternoon I hastened up the drive to the huge doors giving access to the main building, my mind consumed with eager anticipation of the treat in store for me.

I was welcomed into an imposing edifice of pleasing aspect, where the said commodity is mass-produced in a manner with which the general public is all too little acquainted, by the smiling works manager, who offered to conduct me personally on my tour. Willingly accepting his generous invitation, I was ushered along a short corridor, tastefully decorated on either side, into a spacious chamber divided into three sections.

On my left was situated the largest, the wax department, so I was informed. This section was a veritable hive of industry. White-aproned workers of both sexes scurried to and fro bearing large trays of gleaming wax, which were in due course inserted into the roaring furnaces occupying the furthermost side of this department. Once the wax has attained the required degree of malleability, it is deposited to one side for cooling.

We then follow it into the adjoining chamber, the moulding section. Here sit girls busily fashioning the wax into the desired length, thickness and shape of the candle-to-be, guided in their efforts by a life-size model occupying pride of place on every bench, and affectionately referred to as the 'perf', an abbreviation of 'perfect'.

Next after this procedure comes the journey into the wicking room. Here the wax acquires its last stage of perfection. On tables stand enormous jars of cotton wicks. The nimble fingers of the overalled girls can be seen extracting wick after wick from their respective jars and, by their use of bodkins, steering them with machine-like precision down the very centre of the waxen mouldings, leaving a small portion of the wick projecting at the top for lighting purposes.

Each candle thus reaches the high standard of performance aimed at, although a minute proportion of them are found by the eagle-eyed testers to be faultily crafted, or, in the jargon of the candle trade, 'miswicked'. If such is indeed the case (and the meticulous exactitude maintained by the workers reduces these to a very low figure) the defective candles pass to the rewicking bench which, requiring only a small number of operatives, stands in one corner of the wicking department.

The finished products are stacked into bales, roped together, and transported on lorries to the stores for sale to the public. After seeing the despatch department my tour of inspection concluded, and I passed out not a little enlightened into the open air, having complimented the manager on the keenness and splendid efficiency of his staff.

It is to be fervently hoped that I have managed to convey some impression to the reader of the amount of skilful industry that goes into the manufacture of every British candle, and I sincerely trust that, having been apprised of its true merits, the housewife will in future spare a moment to reflect with fond and due appreciation on the little object she is about to light. The candle is playing a magnificent part in these difficult days, and long may it continue doing its fine job of work in the times of peace to come!

This send-up of provincial journalism started as a family joke involving an itinerant vegetable-seller who sold his produce from a donkey-and-cart in North Watford. It dates from 1950.

ISLE OF ROMANCE

Browsing through my local paper last night, a paragraph struck my eye, and I read with absorption how a young couple have settled in a houseboat on the Isle of Birds. Straightaway the gates of Memory were flung open, and recollections came flooding back to mind. I bethought me of a similar event in the dim past, on that selfsame picturesque spot, and wondered how many readers would have been aware of its unique and fascinating history. Truly, the tale I unfold reads like a romantic novelette!

In 1895 or thereabouts, there lived at Capel Park, near Berkhamsted, the aristocratic family of that ilk – Lord Capel, a nobleman of the old school, his wife, a fine stately figure of a woman, and their only daughter, Lady Christabel Capel. She was a shy, unspoilt, artistic girl, who loved to sketch in the spacious grounds of the estate.

It was while sketching the stables one morning that she first encountered James Abbot, a young groom of dashing appearance. It must have been love at first sight, for they were soon meeting secretly and exchanging vows of undying affection. Three months later they eloped, and chose for their honeymoon a charming, out-of-the-way beauty spot on the Grand Union Junction Canal near Hunton Bridge – none other than the Isle of Birds.

Here James Abbot settled with his young bride, and like a modern Crusoe converted a tumbledown shack into a sturdy home, using timber from the plentiful island trees. Here they dwelt, poor but happy, for the girl's proud parents had immediately disowned her when her escapade and unsuitable marriage were discovered. James, ably assisted by his loving girl-wife, tilled the rich soil and made a scanty living from his market produce, which he hawked through the streets of rural Watford.

This idyllic existence lasted until 1899, when James, chafing at the pleasant but unexciting life on the island, answered the call to the colours and went off to fight the Boer. He gained instant success as a soldier, was commissioned and won his spurs at Colenso. His prowess in the field was soon recognised, and he was promoted major at Spion Kop. The fearless Britisher, with an old clay pipe clenched always in his teeth, became a legend in the Boer Camp, striking terror in their craven hearts.

The war reached its climax in the year 1901, when a small force under Major Abbot surprised the main strength of the Boers at the village of Bardokidogo. The Major led his men in a cavalry charge into the midst of the enemy, routing them utterly. For this gallant and decisive exploit (for it marked the turning point of the war) Major Abbot was awarded the Victoria Cross and a knighthood. How proud was his faraway spouse when with trembling fingers and fluttering heart she opened the official envelope from the War Office and drank in the joyous news.

The war over, the victorious warriors returned in triumph, and the bronzed major was welcomed with open arms by his adoring wife. Later they attended a special investiture at Buckingham Palace, and Christabel's heart swelled with emotion as the sovereign pinned the coveted medal on her man's chest. A tap of the sword, and her husband rose Sir James. The knight and his lady returned to their humble home in a blaze of glory.

Lord Capel found himself being congratulated on his fine son-in-law, and had perforce to relent his harsh decision. He and his wife begged Christabel to return to their ancestral seat, but she too had her pride. Her eyes flashing fire, she informed her parents that she preferred to stay by her husband's side in their simple dwelling and chosen station, and the rebuff put paid to any hope of reconciliation.

In the peaceful seclusion of their island retreat they lived contentedly, and the figure of the knight was often to be seen, trusty pipe in mouth, vending his produce from a gaily-painted donkey-drawn cart, inscribed with the intriguing word 'BARDOKIDOGO'. Their wants were few, for they lived only for each other, and their humble shack was a palace where love held sway.

Christabel's courage was equal to that of her husband. On a famous occasion one of their goats missed its footing and sank into the deep waters of the canal. Without a moment's hesitation the gallant lady plunged in and struggled with the animal to the safety of the bank. Passers-by on the towpath stopped to applaud her heroic deed.

In 1939 the knight, now old and grizzled, but still of upright bearing, died and was given a splendid funeral in Watford with full military honours. His last wish was to be laid to rest in the soil he loved so well. His sorrowing widow could not bear the solitude of the island without the company of her mate, and removed to Tunbridge Wells. The shack fell into disrepair, while weeds and tangled scrub ran riot over the deserted island. Ere long the only reminder of their sojourn there was the name given to the mooring-place, which rejoiced in the title of 'Lady Capel's Wharf'.

But the Abbots had stamped their character indelibly on that lovely spot, and in my mind's eye I see them still, sitting of an evening in the deepening dusk, Sir James puffing at a short clay, and Christabel's nimble fingers painting or knitting, forming a charming scene of tranquil content. One can only hope that the present inhabitants of this romantic isle may enjoy the blissful beatitude of their distinguished predecessors.

As a young diplomat in Ceylon, one of my delights was to satirise the Soviet system. A friendly local editor with a great sense of humour was very cooperative in printing my japes with a distinctive byline. This one was published in the *Times of Ceylon* in October 1961.

TAX RELIEF FOR THE 'LITTLE MAN'

MOSCOW, 7 October (Royter)

Following the announcement that Soviet dwarfs are to be made free of income tax, the Chairman of the State Planning Commission, Mr A.N. Kosygin, has published details of the Russian 'Lilliputi', broken down by age and sex.

It is decreed by the Supreme Soviet that a dwarf is a person over 21 who has not reached a height of 1.25 metres (about 4 ft 2 in). The latest census shows that there are 15,663 registered male dwarfs and 1,371 females in the Soviet Union. Eighty per cent are in the age group 21–30, fifteen per cent between 31 and 40, and five per cent over 40. The maximum age of 56 was attained by a dwarf who returned from Nome, Alaska, in 1923.

A survey carried out at the time of the census reveals that 38.6 per cent of male dwarfs attributed their lack of height to smoking Caucasian tobacco, 28.9 per cent to nuclear fallout, 13.2 per cent to living in a low-roofed house, 5.7 per cent to looking at Sputniks, and 1.8 per cent to 'the Government'. The remainder said 'Don't know'.

The Secretary of the All-Union Committee of Working Dwarfs, Mr V. Manikin, has welcomed the news that male dwarfs will be able to draw their old age pensions at 45 and females at 40. He added that his organisation would continue their campaign for equal pension rights. At present Soviet dwarfs receive only two-thirds of the national rates.

In 1971 an economics course provided the stimulus for this satire on professional methodology and jargon. My genial tutor, Professor Harry Johnson of the LSE, liked the idea and tried to get it published, without success.

ACADEMICS AND THE KEYNESIAN-FRIEDMANITE CONTROVERSY

Some university economists have argued that the extreme form of monetarism advocated by Milton Friedman was not the answer to Britain's economic decline. Will this mean a return to the fiscal policies of Maynard Keynes? The argument between proponents of the two schools of thought continues unabated.

It is not the purpose of this article to discuss the relative merits of the Keynesian and Friedmanite theories. Rather, we shall seek to determine whether there is any point of correspondence between them which, *ceteris paribus*, might provide the basis for an appropriate formula for the sustained economic growth of the United Kingdom over the next decade.

Since the most sophisticated statistical approaches appear to give only inconclusive results, we shall investigate whether any academic correlation may be observed. We start, then, by examining the impact which the two theories have had on academic circles in the United Kingdom.

A study of the literature shows that, as one might expect, Cambridge has wholeheartedly accepted the Keynesian hypothesis. Oxford is perhaps not so fully committed, but clearly shows a marginal propensity to Keynes. In the capital, on the other hand, at the London School of Economics and the London Business School, the Friedmanite doctrine appears to have made a considerable impression on the younger academics.

Having obtained these three readings, we can proceed to plot them by normal graphic means to see whether there is any convergence. On the basis of given data, we obtain what may be termed the 'theory preference curves' illustrated in Fig. 1.

It may be assumed that the point at which the theory preference curves are in equilibrium represents a point of academic concurrence on the optimum mix of economic policies in the United Kingdom context. This conclusion can now be tested empirically by superimposing our graph over a map of southern England; point MK is revealed as the new town of Milton Keynes.

Now that we have established the geographical location of our point of equilibrium, the academic picture becomes clear. For Milton Keynes is the site of the Open University founded in 1969, and therefore the most modern seat of learning in the United Kingdom. It also has roots in the past, for it was 'built in the grounds of Walton Hall, a late Georgian mansion in a parkland setting on the banks of the River Ouzel'.[1]

At this stage of our enquiry it is essential to identify the theory preference of the Open University, whose economists are not given to polemical public statements. To do this we shall need to examine the views of the Head of the Economics Department, Professor F.S. Brooman, as set out in his standard economics textbook.[2]

In his discussion of the quantity theory of money, Brooman refers to the reformulation of the classical theory which is attributed to economists at Cambridge: $M = kY$.

Significantly, the elements of this equation have a familiar look. We find that Milton Friedman's attachment to the quantity theory as a policy guide[3] and Keynes' original ideas on the role of the quantity theory[4] can be employed to develop the analysis which, in the light of our previous argument, may give some further insight into a resolution of the controversy.

Redefining M to mean Milton and $\frac{1}{k}$ as Keynes, by simple algebra we can render the expression to give: $Mk = Y$ (where Y stands for the gross national product). In other words, maximising Milton Keynes automatically means maximising the rate of growth of GNP in the country as a whole.

Milton Keynes thus stands as a symbol of growth in the

United Kingdom. By 1980 the number of students will have reached 50,000. The new town itself is set on attaining its ambitious target of a 250,000 population by the end of the century.

The forward-looking attitude of Milton Keynes is summed up by the simple anagram which the Development Corporation no doubt had in mind when they chose its name: Money Tinkles. And the central location of Milton Keynes in terms of the national economy is reflected in its 'perfect position halfway between London and Birmingham on the M1, the A5 and the main line from Euston to the North'.

The implications of this result are not, of course, merely geographical. It would be ludicrous to suggest that resources should be poured into the new town of Milton Keynes beyond the point of diminishing returns. But it certainly should give us cause to ponder very carefully the writings of its leading economic pundit.

Professor Brooman writes that both fiscal and monetary measures may be unable to control the economy, and that governments may occasionally be quite powerless to do anything at all to correct undesirable tendencies in the general level of activity and prices in the economy.[5]

Such a conclusion is not, of course, in the least original. It is epitomised in the laissez-faire attitude of the classical economists. Such originality as could conceivably be claimed for the result as presented here must lie entirely with the novel application of multi-disciplinary techniques we have used in an attempt to resolve the current debate on the role of monetary and fiscal policies.

One might conclude that the appropriate policy recommendations arising from this study are neither a reversion to laissez-faire, nor an adoption of the more modern approach via an incomes policy, but a judicious blend of the two. But whether one takes a further step from this conclusion is very largely a matter of political taste, on which economists are precluded by the discipline of their science from passing judgment.

REFERENCES

1. *Commonwealth Universities Yearbook* (1970).
2. F.S. Brooman, *Macro-Economics* (4th Edition, 1970).
3. M. Friedman, *Studies in the Quantity Theory of Money* (1956).
4. J.M. Keynes, *The General Theory of Employment, Interest and Money* (1936).
5. F.S. Brooman, op. cit., p.283.

Fig. 1 – The Theory Preference Curves

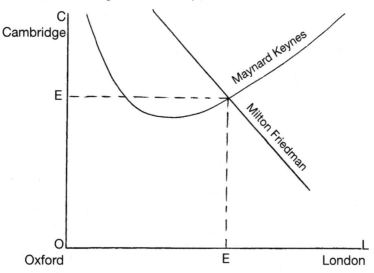

NOTES

The conventional U shape of the Keynesian curve is no more than a geometric illustration of a natural regression towards the mean as departure from the ancient seats of learning at Oxford and Cambridge involves a decline in marginal utility with the approach of the capital. Conversely, the linearity of the Friedman function reflects the proportionate increase in acceptability of his doctrine in non-U institutions.

Two further observations in the field of economics.

TB OR NOT TB?

The student of economics must grasp at the outset that an association between two factors does not necessarily involve a causal relationship. Let us take as an example the so-called 'Arizona Anomaly'.

Health statistics show that Arizona, which has the healthiest climate in the United States, also has the highest rate of tuberculosis per head of population.

The reason is not that the unfortunate sufferers have contracted the disease in Arizona, but that they have travelled there from all over the USA to be cured of it. In other words, there has been what the economists call a shift in the pattern of consumption.

LIQUIDITY PREFERENCE

In analysing the motives for holding resources in money, we start from the assumption that everybody will wish money to retain its value over a period of time – the pound must be worth a pound.

Other factors to be taken into consideration are the rate of interest (i), the volume of transactions (t), and the aggregate income (y). From these we can construct the equation:

$$£ = 1 \text{ quid (i) ty.}$$

Economists refer to this as the liquidity preference theory.

This essay in bad taste was published by the *Spectator* in August 1991.

BLOOMSBURY BOOKLIST

The 50th anniversary of the death of Virginia Woolf this year has generated fresh interest in the life and works of the revered prose stylist. More readers will be encouraged to tackle the mysteries of her craft; others will seek enlightenment on the literary and social phenomenon known as the Bloomsbury Group. There already exists a bewildering array of scholarly material on these themes produced by the Woolf industry. Whatever view you may take on the great Lupine controversy – pro or anti-Woolf – you will wish to keep up with dinner conversation in the smartest circles. Here are some of the most important books recommended for study:

ALBEE, Edward: *Who's Who in Virginia Woolf.*
BELL, Quentin: *Travails with my Aunt.*
BELL, Vanessa: *A Feast of Stephens.*
BETJEMAN, John: *Twilight on Virginia Water.*
BLAKE, Michael: *Dances with Woolfs.*
BROOKE, Rupert: *Carry me Back to Old Virginny.*
BYATT, Antonia: *Virginia in the Garden.*
CARRINGTON, Dora: *Love in Bloomsbury.*
CARTER, Angela: *The Company of Woolfs.*
ELIOT, Thomas Stearns: *The Sacred Woolf.*
FRY, Roger: *Virgin by Design.*
GARNETT, David: *Lady into Woolf.*
GLENDINNING, Victoria: *Vita, Violet, Virginia and Vanessa.*
HESSE, Hermann: *Stephen-Woolf.*
HUGHES, Richard: *The Woolf in the Attic.*
JOYCE, James: *Bloom's Beret.*
LAWRENCE, David Herbert: *Virginia and the Gypsy.*
MANSFIELD, Katherine: *Cry Woolf, and Other Stories.*
MORRELL, Ottoline: *The Circle in the Square – a Bloomsbury Diary.*

NICOLSON, Harold: *The Congress of Virginia.*
NICOLSON, Nigel: *Portrait of a Mirage – the Elusive Virginia.*
PRITCHETT, Victor Sawdon: *A Woolf at the Door.*
SACKVILLE-WEST, Vita: *Virginia Creeper.*
SHOLOKHOV, Mikhail: *Virginia's Soil Upturned.*
SMITH, Stevie: *Not Waving but Drowning – Imagery of Virginia Woolf.*
STRACHEY, Lytton: *Eminent Virginians.*
WALTON, William Turner: *The Wise Virginia.*
WEBB, Mary: *Woolf's Bane.*
WELLS, Herbert George: *The War of the Woolfs.*
WISTER, Owen: *The Virginian.*
WOOLF, Leonard: *Virginia in the Jungle.*
WOOLF, Virginia: *The Wolves.*

An attempt at satire rejected by *Private Eye*.

REPORTER SACKED FOR INFAMOUS CONDUCT

By Our Media Correspondent

John Trusty, a junior reporter on the *Daily Smut*, was sacked yesterday for 'bringing the press into disrepute'.

As editor Gus McPorney explained to a crowd of indignant hacks in El Vino's: 'The lad had to go. I caught him in the act of checking the facts of a story. It's the worst case of ethics I've come across in 25 years in Fleet Street.

'We've got to put a stop to this sort of thing before it takes hold. Just imagine what would happen if busy journalists followed this lead – we'd never be able to give our readers the juicy stories they expect.

'Trusty has apologised for his aberration, and promised that it wouldn't happen again. But I can't afford to take the risk, and I told him I felt compelled to sack him for his own good, and for the sake of the profession.'

The Father of the Chapel, R. Scrawler, backed the editor's decision. 'The boy's been through training courses and ought to know better,' he commented. 'He's broken the fundamental rule of journalistic practice, and a proud tradition which we have fought hard to uphold against interfering busybodies.

'He's guilty of the kind of unauthorised innovation that we can't accept in our profession. It's appalling that he's set such a bad example to our younger members.'

Trusty is understood to be seeking a post of Information Officer in MAFF.

TRANSLATIONS

These two fragments of Latin verse, translated in 1944, were found in a school exercise book.

LUCRETIUS

De Rerum Natura

Sic rerum summa novatur
Semper, et inter se mortales mutua vivunt.
Augescunt aliae gentes, aliae minuuntur,
Inque brevi spatio mutantur saecla animantum
Et quasi cursores vitai lampada tradunt.

Thus the sum of things
Is constantly replenished. Humans live
By mutual dependence on each other.
Some nations wax in power, while others wane;
In little time the living generations
Change, and like runners in a relay race,
Hand on the torch of life.

VIRGIL

Aeneid

En Priamus. 'Sunt hic etiam sua praemia laudi;
Sunt lacrimae rerum et mentem mortalia tangunt.
Solve metus; feret haec aliquam tibi fama salutem'.

Lo, Priam speaks.
'Virtues shall be rewarded even here.
There is a sadness at the heart of things,
And worldly matters can affect the mind.
Dispel thy fears; the fame thou hast achieved
Shall bring thee some salvation'.

Claude Rouget de Lisle (1760–1836) wrote his stirring patriotic song in 1792. This version was a schoolboy's tribute to our French allies, to celebrate the liberation of Paris in 1944.

LA MARSEILLAISE

Rouget de Lisle

Allons, enfants de la patrie,
Le jour de gloire est arrivé!
Contre nous de la tyrannie
L'étendard sanglant est levé
L'étendard sanglant est levé.
Entendez-vous dans les campagnes
Mugir ces féroces soldats,
Ils viennent jusque dans nos bras
Egorger nos fils et nos compagnes.
Aux armes, citoyens! Formez vos bataillons!
Marchons! Marchons!
Qu'un sang impur abreuve nos sillons.

Arise, ye children of our nation,
The day of glory now is here.
As the tyrants wreak devastation
See their bloodstained banners appear,
See their bloodstained banners appear.
Can you not hear our woods and waters
Resound with the cries of these hordes,
Who approach us ready with their swords
To destroy our sons and wives and daughters.
To arms, ye citizens! In battle ranks parade!
March on, march on!
Let their vile blood flow deep o'er field and glade.

An exercise in translating a classic of German literature, done in 1945 before I had ever heard of Beethoven's Ninth Symphony.

AN DIE FREUDE

Friedrich von Schiller

Freude, schöner Götterfunken,
Tochter aus Elysium,
Wir betreten feuertrunken,
Himmlische, dein Heiligtum.
Deiner Zauber binden wieder,
Was die Mode streng geteilt,
Alle Menschen werden Brüder
Wo dein sanfter Flügel weilt.
Seid umschlungen, Millionen!
Diesen Kuss der ganzen Welt!
Brüder – überm Sternenzelt
Muss ein lieber Vater wohnen.

ODE TO JOY

Joy, thy godlike radiance spreading,
Daughter of Elysian line,
Dazed by rapture, we are treading,
Sacred one, thy holy shrine.
Let thy spell unite all others
Rent apart by worldly things,
All mankind becoming brothers
Sheltered by thy gentle wings.
May our millions be surrounded
By this universal love!
Brothers – in the stars unbounded
Our dear Father reigns above.

Charles, Duke of Orleans (1394–1465) was taken prisoner at Agincourt in 1415 and spent 25 years in captivity in Pontefract Castle before being ransomed. During this time he wrote some of his finest poetry. This poem and the translation were published in *Christmas Crackers*, an anthology edited by John Julius Norwich (Penguin, 1982). They were later set to music, to be sung in either language (see under 'Songs').

RONDEAU DE PRINTEMPS

Charles D'Orléans

Le temps a laissié son manteau
De vent, de froidure et de pluye,
Et s'est vestu de brouderie,
De soleil luyant, cler et beau.
Il n'y a beste, ne oyseau
Qu'en son jargon ne chant ou crie:
Le temps a laissié son manteau
De vent, de froidure et de pluye.
Rivière, fontaine et ruisseau
Portent, en livrée jolie,
Gouttes d'argent d'orfavrerie,
Chascun s'abille de nouveau.
Le temps a laissié son manteau.

SPRING WEATHER

Old Weather's shed his sombre shroud
Of wind and rain and bitter cold,
And let his broidery unfold
Of shining sunlight, clear and proud.
The birds and beasts all sing aloud,
Each giving tongue in his own mould;
Old Weather's shed his sombre shroud
Of wind and rain and bitter cold.
River and stream and fountain loud
Are wearing as their livery bold
Jewels of silver and of gold,
All is with raiment new endowed.
Old Weather's shed his sombre shroud.

This fine sonnet by Pierre de Ronsard (1524–1585) haunted me for years. I finally got around to translating it in 2001.

POUR HÉLÈNE

Pierre de Ronsard

Quand vous serez bien vieille, au soir, à la chandelle,
Assise aupres du feu, devidant et filant,
Direz chantant mes vers, en vous esmerveillant:
Ronsard me celebroit du temps que j'estois belle.

Lors vous n'aurez servante oyant telle nouvelle,
Desja sous le labeur à demy sommeillant,
Qui au bruit de mon nom me s'aille resveillant,
Benissant vostre nom de louange immortelle.

Je seray sous la terre, et, fantome sans os,
Par les ombres myrteux je prendray mon repos:
Vous serez au fouyer une vieille accroupie,

Regrettant mon amour et vostre fier desdain.
Vivez, si m'en croyez, n'attendez à demain:
Cueillez des aujourd'huy les roses de la vie.

TO HELEN

When you are old, at eve, by candle rays,
In fireside seat, on thread and spinning bent,
You'll sing my verse, and say in wonderment:
'Ronsard revered me in my fairer days'.

No serving-maid who heard that lovely phrase,
Already half asleep from labours spent,
Upon my name, could help but rise intent,
Blessing your name with immemorial praise.

I shall be deep in earth, a boneless shade,
Taking my rest in myrtle-scented glade;
Crouched by your hearth, you will be old and grey,
Your pride that spurned my love recalled in sorrow.
Live now, I say – don't tarry till tomorrow,
For life's sweet roses must be plucked today.

The Fables of La Fontaine (1621–1695) are deceptively simple, but make their point forcibly. This translation was made in 1977.

LE CORBEAU ET LE RENARD

Jean de la Fontaine

Maître Corbeau, sur un arbre perché,
Tenait en son bec un fromage;
Maître Renard, par l'odeur alléché,
Lui tint à peu près ce langage.
'Eh bonjour, Monsieur du Corbeau,
Que vous êtes joli, que vous me semblez beau!
Sans mentir, si votre ramage
Se rapporte à votre plumage,
Vous êtes le Phénix des hôtes de ces bois!'
A ces mots le corbeau ne se sent pas de joie,
Et pour montrer sa belle voix
Il ouvre un large bec, laisse tomber sa proie.
Le renard s'en saisit, et dit: 'Mon bon monsieur,
Apprenez que tout flatteur
Vit au dépens de celui qui l'écoute.
Cette leçon vaut bien un fromage, sans doute'.
Le corbeau, honteux et confus,
Jura, mais un peu tard, qu'on ne l'y prendrait plus.

THE CROW AND THE FOX

The crow, perched high among the trees,
Held in his beak a tasty cheese.
The fox, attracted by the scent,
Thought he would try some blandishment.
'Good day, Sir Crow', the villain said,
'How fine your eye, how sleek your head.
I swear that, if your singing voice
Matches your plumage, rich and choice,
You are the Phoenix of our woods and skies!'
The foolish crow, ecstatically proud,
And all too keen to raise his voice aloud,
Then opened wide his beak and dropped the prize.
The sly fox grabbed it, saying: 'My dear sir,
You've got to learn that every flatterer
Battens on those whom honeyed words may please.
That lesson's surely worth a piece of cheese'.
The humbled crow resolved – a trifle late –
He'd never fall again for such a bait.

The poems by Charles Baudelaire (1821–1867) in *Les Fleurs du Mal* have an irresistible fascination. One of my favourites was translated in 1995.

L'ALBATROS

Baudelaire

Souvent, pour s'amuser, les hommes d'équipage
Prennent des albatros, vastes oiseaux des mers,
Qui suivent, indolents compagnons de voyage,
Le navire glissant sur les gouffres amers.

A peine les ont-ils déposés sur les planches,
Que ces rois de l'azur, maladroits et honteux,
Laissent piteusement leurs grandes ailes blanches
Comme des avirons traîner à côté d'eux.

Ce voyageur ailé, comme il est gauche et veule!
Lui, naguère si beau, qu'il est comique et laid!
L'un agace son bec avec un brûle-gueule,
L'autre mime, en boitant, l'infirme qui volait.

Le Poète est semblable au prince des nuées
Qui hante la tempête et se rit de l'archer;
Exilé sur le sol au milieu des huées,
Ses ailes de géant l'empêchent de marcher.

THE ALBATROSS

Just for amusement, deck-hands like to trap
The albatrosses, monsters of the ocean,
Whose lazy pinions scarcely seem to flap,
Yet match the vessel in its gliding motion.

No sooner have they fetched these aerial kings
Upon the deck when, shorn of grace and pride,
They pitifully let their great white wings
Like useless oar-blades, droop on either side.

The soaring bird, in clumsy disarray,
Once beautiful, becomes a laughing-stock;
His beak is tickled with an ancient clay,
His crippled gait becomes a seaman's mock.

So too the poet. Regal in the clouds,
He braves both storm and foes with easy mirth.
But once brought low, amid the noisy crowds,
His very genius roots him to the earth.

René Sully-Prudhomme (1839–1907), one of the French Symbolist poets, was awarded the Nobel Prize for Literature in 1901. His best-known poem – a little gem – was translated in 1998.

LE VASE BRISÉ

Sully-Prudhomme

*Le vase où meurt cette verveine
D'un coup d'éventail fut fêlé;
Le coup dut l'effleurer à peine.
Aucun bruit ne l'a révélé.*

*Mais la légère meurtrissure,
Mordant le cristal chaque jour,
D'une marche invisible et sûre
En a fait lentement le tour.*

*Son eau fraîche a fui goutte à goutte,
Le suc des fleurs s'est épuisé;
Personne encore ne s'en doute.
N'y touchez pas, il est brisé.*

*Souvent aussi la main qu'on aime
Effleurant le coeur, le meurtrit;
Puis le coeur se fend de lui-même,
La fleur de son amour périt.*

*Toujours intact aux yeux du monde,
Il sent croître et pleurer tout bas
Sa blessure fine et profonde.
Il est brisé, n'y touchez pas.*

THE BROKEN VASE

The vase where this verbena died,
Brushed by a fan, was lightly cracked.
The gentle blow scarce grazed the side;
No sound was heard to mark the act.

And yet the bruise, however slight,
Gnawing the crystal day by day,
With stealthy progress, out of sight,
Around the circle made its way.

The precious water trickled out,
The flower's sap was drained too much;
No one can any longer doubt,
It has been broken, do not touch.

Sometimes the hand of one adored
Grazing the heart, may leave it bruised;
The heart cracks of its own accord,
And flowering love will die unused.

This casual wound, so fine, so deep,
Though still unseen, unknown, unspoken,
Grows in the heart and makes it weep.
O do not touch, it has been broken.

While staying with a friend in Normandy in August 1996 I was shown this remarkable poem by an elderly lady in Bordeaux, who wished to see an English translation of her work. This was the result.

L'EUCALYPTUS

Claire Bertaincourt

L'eucalyptus se déshabille
Il va assister au concert;
Et quitte sa cape de guenilles
Pour revêtir chaperon clair.

Va-t-il écouter le choral
Du groupe de chardonnerets?
Ou ouïr le chant de carnaval
De cet oiseau si guilleret?

Tenture de ciel, tenture de bleu
Au loin j'entends carillonner;
Est-ce l'entrée d'oiseau de feu
Tout d'incarnat damasquiné?

Seule, apparaît une hirondelle
Avec son tout petit flûteau;
'Eucalyptus' amoureux d'elle
A su quitter ses oripeaux.

THE EUCALYPTUS

The eucalyptus changes dress
To listen to the singing wood;
Off with its cloak of raggedness,
Better to wear its brightest hood.

Now will the solemn choral voice
Of swarming goldfinches be heard?
Or festive singing be the choice
Of such a gay and sprightly bird?

Against the cloth of azure sky
Is heard a far-off pealing chime;
Is it the firebird passing by
Enamelled with a blush sublime?

A single swallow flies above
To raise its tiny fluting song;
The eucalyptus, full of love,
Has shed the rags it wore so long.

BALLADES

My first entry to a literary competition, a ballade on a given refrain, took second prize in the *Spectator* in July 1951.

BALLADE OF DEAD POETS

Though Byron reigns supreme at Harrow
And Athens worships at his shrine,
Eton, whose mind is somewhat narrow,
Would gladly see his fame decline.
Italians reckon Keats divine,
The counterpart of Botticelli
In colour, feeling and design –
But Old Etonians like Shelley.

Canada deems 'I shot an arrow'
Longfellow's best. The Argentine
In Wordsworth finds a 'winsome marrow',
And loves the 'lesser celandine'.
China reads Marlowe's mighty line;
Milton is popular in Delhi;
Paris considers Pope is fine –
But Old Etonians like Shelley.

'Molly Malone' and famous barrow
Are heard when Dublin students dine;
Says Edinburgh, 'Braes of Yarrow',
While Cardiff chooses 'Clementine'.
Harvard and Yale sing 'Adeline',
And men of Bristol chorus 'Nellie';
Heidelberg sticks to 'Wacht am Rhein',
But Old Etonians like Shelley.

Envoi

Prince, do not think me asinine,
Nor shake with laughter in your belly.
Who can disprove this view of mine
But Old Etonians like Shelley?

In 1954, East-West talks, Billy Graham, equal pay, MCC v West Indies – gloomy prospects providing an ambivalent title.

BALLADE OF SOME HOPES

The talks have ended in Berlin,
Reason and peace have won the day;
A brighter era will begin
Tomorrow, so the experts say.
Diplomacy has found a way
To bring together East and West;
The future is no longer grey –
And everything is for the best.

With flashing eye and jutting chin
A zealot from the USA
Has come to lead us out of sin
By urging folk to sing and pray.
Roll up, all those who tend to stray,
For sing-songs soothe the troubled breast;
Salvation waits at Harringay –
And everything is for the best.

Unyielding, sternly masculine,
The Chancellor has stood at bay
For years. At last he's given in
And granted women equal pay.
Inspired to do as well as they
The English men have won a test;
Even the press applauds their play –
And everything is for the best.

Envoi

My Lord! Let nothing you dismay
(Rumours of discord and unrest);
Prosperity has come to stay –
And everything is for the best.

Nowadays crime reports usually end with 'A man is helping police with their enquiries'. Things were different in 1964.

BALLADE OF SUBSEQUENT CONFINEMENT

This was the crime of the year,
Exceeding all powers of invention.
Seems that the gang had got clear
With loot of enormous dimension.
The Yard gave it all their attention
Till some of the swag was regained;
Their efforts allowed no suspension –
Later a man was detained.

Curious case of a Peer
Attending his Party's convention,
Found in a barrel of beer,
Although he was known for abstention.
In fact, it had been his contention
That drunks should be publicly caned
(A view that could lead to dissension) –
Later a man was detained.

Striking a city with fear
A killer defied apprehension;
Corpse after corpse would appear
With markings too horrid to mention.
So great was the general tension
The head of the force was constrained
To pray for divine intervention –
Later a man was detained.

Envoi

My Lord, I submit that prevention
Is better than crime unrestrained.
I ask for preventive detention –
Later a man was detained.

A literary competition in 1984 asked for a ballade on a given refrain – the theme of suicidal despair.

BALLADE OF MISERY

As Chesterton informed us long ago,
The ice is breaking up on every side.
The teachers have decided to go slow,
The miners' pickets can't be pacified.
A Russian team has humbled England's pride,
Our cricketers have hit a losing streak;
Two leading entertainers have just died;
I tried to kill myself three times last week.

Deep floods have followed on the heels of snow
To devastate the town where I reside;
A bolt of lightning struck my bungalow;
Two ships have foundered in the massive tide.
My maiden aunt has just been certified,
Thieves have got in and snatched my prize antique.
A maniac has stabbed a lovely bride;
I tried to kill myself three times last week.

In spirit I have never been so low,
And balk at things once taken in my stride.
When told of my redundancy, the blow
Was too much for me. I sat down and cried.
Wars and disasters flourish far and wide;
The dollar's high, the pound is up the creek,
My shares have shown a catastrophic slide;
I tried to kill myself three times last week.

Envoi

My Lord, the horrors cannot be denied –
Whichever way you look, the future's bleak.
The only remedy is suicide;
I tried to kill myself three times last week.

124

LIGHT VERSE

This is the earliest surviving verse effort by the author, written at Watford Grammar School in 1938 as an animal poem. Though showing a distressing lack of knowledge of farm life, it nevertheless has a certain pathos.

THE OLD COW

Once in a meadow there lived an old cow
Who played with the calves all day;
But alas, the poor cow doesn't play with them now
Because she has passed away.

The creature died from loss of breath,
She could not stand the pace;
But even in the chill of death
A smile still creased her face.

A grounding in the English poets apparently inspired this school-boy sonnet, published in *The Fullerian* in 1943. It has a rather pompous quality very much at variance with the author's reputation for unruly behaviour which almost led to his expulsion from Watford Grammar School

COUNTRY JOYS

When the time comes that I from work retire
(If 'tis my fortune this should ever be),
When I from City toil and cares am free
Should I be wealthy, 'twill be my desire
A cottage in the country to acquire,
Therein to dwell with wife for company
And end my days in peaceful luxury.
Then in the evening, by a roaring fire,
Reclining in a comfortable armchair,
Smoking a pipe (a present from my wife),
I'll see old London with its smoky air,
Its noisy turmoil and incessant strife;
Then will I sigh, and thankfully declare
'How pleasant are the joys of country life'.

This sonnet dating from 1943 was recently unearthed in a school exercise book.

ON AN EMPTY HOUSE

It stands, a gaunt and crumbling pile of stone,
Surrounded by a drear expanse of moor.
No mason could its former pride restore;
The elements have claimed it for their own.
The gravelled drive is thickly overgrown,
For years no man has trod inside the door.
This, the famed haunt of lords in days of yore,
Is now uncared-for, undesired, unknown.
No more do parties gather for the grouse,
Nor awe-struck tourists pay their curious call;
Where once a marquis slept reclines a mouse,
In fine apartments loathsome creatures crawl.
This dismal fate awaits a mighty house –
Today it stands; tomorrow it may fall.

During World War II, when all sweets were strictly rationed on points, bars of chocolate on display in confectioners' shops were actually small blocks of wood in a manufacturer's wrapper. This poem was written in 1944 after reading Robert W. Service.

THE BALLAD OF SIX-GUN PETE

Down the dusty street rode Six-Gun Pete,
It was plain he was in a bad mood.
His belt was drawn in, he was terribly thin –
For a week he had tasted no food.

He came to a stop and went into a shop,
His hands at his hips by his guns.
With a desperate look some milk chocolate he took,
A sausage, and six currant buns.

With enough for a feed he sprang onto his steed
And rode off as fast as he could.
When clear of the town the outlaw climbed down
And led the horse into a wood.

The sausage he swallowed, two currant buns followed,
The others he shared with his horse.
Then he picked up the sweet, a spectacular treat
That he'd saved as a tasty last course.

He eyed with delight the mouth-watering sight,
Then the wrapper he started to peel.
But his teeth got a jar when the chocolate bar
Turned out to be fashioned of deal.

There's a moral, you know, to this story of woe,
And I hope you'll agree it's a good 'un;
When stuck for a meal and some foodstuffs you steal,
Make sure they are real, and not wooden.

Memories of a particularly unfortunate camping trip in 1948 found expression in these verses.

PASTORALE

Campers once selected
Insects' paradise.
Tent was soon erected;
Enter bugs and lice.

Midge and gnat descended
Swiftly on the camp.
Then the murmur ended –
Jaws began to champ.

Moth arrived a-flutter
Tempted by the greens;
Worm explored the butter,
Caterpillar, beans.

Centipede and spider
Battened on the ham;
Hornet guzzled cider,
Wasp invaded jam.

Horsefly tackled brisket,
Cockroach munched the steak;
Earwig nibbled biscuit,
Ant demolished cake.

Slug attacked potato,
Cranefly gobbled cheese;
Lettuce fell a prey to
Woolly aphides.

Beetle browsed on bacon
Snail devoured eggs;
Sugar lumps were taken
Gripped in furry legs.

Grasshopper and cricket
Swarmed around the tent;
Campers could not stick it –
Packed their kit and went.

These verses are based on a remark made by a publican's son, overheard at a country inn in 1950, which reminded me of the boisterous music hall songs of the late Victorian period. The actual musical setting was made in 1995.

I CAN'T GET FAT LIKE FATHER

My father serves behind the bar
Down at the 'Blue Horizon';
He's got the biggest pot by far
That ever you've set eyes on.
Now I should like to have a tum
Like Dad's, or even bigger,
But if I drank till Kingdom Come
I'd keep my dainty figure.

Father! Father!
I can't get fat like father.
Father! Father!
I'd like to be like Dad.
Though beer tastes good, without a doubt,
It hasn't got the lather,
So I drink stout to blow me out
But I can't get fat like father.

The other night the Mayor came in
To have his weekly tonic;
He murmured as he sipped his gin
'My indigestion's chronic.
Although in limb I'm very sound
The wind gives me damnation.
I'd gladly give a thousand pound
To have *your* corporation'.

Father! Father!
He can't get fat like father.
Father! Father!
He'd like to be like Dad.
He always drinks a glass of gin
Because, you see, he'd rather;
But drinking gin just keeps him thin
And he can't get fat like father.

A schoolmate well versed in the Augustan style composed an admirable sonnet to twin girls of his acquaintance, beginning: 'Twin paragons of cunning Nature's art!' This prompted a sonnet of a rather different kind.

TO AN OLD PAIR OF TROUSERS

Twin paragons of cunning tailor's art!
Who surely framed thee (nor his wish was vain)
E'en to amaze the world's admiring heart
That he could twice perfection thus attain.
With mingled pain and pride I pay my thanks
To thee, old friends, whose honest sturdy cloth
Protected well these feeble spindly shanks,
Withstanding yet the ravage of the moth.
In winter's frost and tepid summer worn,
Thy sterling worth outscorned the vilest weather;
And oft, when rudely ripped by nail or thorn,
The nimble seamstress drew thy threads together.
Now ends our close attachment through the years –
Thy strength dissolved in tears, and mine in tears.

While on holiday in Barbados in 1983 I was inspired by the island's beauty to write a romantic ballad in the style of an Edwardian parlour song. Words and music came to me simultaneously.

BENEATH THE BAJAN MOON

At close of day the palm trees sway
As shadows fall on still lagoon;
A spicy breeze caresses trees
Beneath the Bajan moon.

The breakers roar along the shore
To surge and shimmer on the dune.
The tropic night is bathed in light
Beneath the Bajan moon.

Magic island of Barbados,
Safe from tempests and tornados;
May your beauty ever be
Shining in the Carib Sea.

The steel guitars play to the stars
While tender voices softly croon,
And lovers kiss in secret bliss
Beneath the Bajan moon.
'Neath the Bajan moon.

This verse had its genesis at a concert in Accra, Ghana in 1985 given by the famous American jazz pianist, Memphis Slim. During the interval I scribbled the lyric of a New Orleans-type blues on the back of my programme and showed it him. He then gave an impromptu rendering of it, to the amazement of the audience. The lyric was set to music by the author in 1996.

BROMLEY BLUES

I feel so miserable, I gotta get out of town,
Yeah, I'm so miserable, I wanna leave this town,
'Cos the man I love, he's gone and let me down.

We loved so sweetly, couldn't bear to be apart,
Used to love so sweetly, we couldn't be apart,
But he walked out on me, and broke my poor old heart.

One of these mornings I'm gonna catch that train,
Tomorrow morning, I'll be on that train,
And this old town won't see my face again.

An acrostic verse dedicated to two good friends who celebrated their silver wedding in Accra in May 1986.

A SILVER SONNET

Pamela came to Ghana, sweet sixteen,
And saw an engineer beneath the palms.
No doubts assailed her, no uneasy qualms
Deterred her from the path that she had seen.
Michael, at first amused and mystified
By this young creature, soon became enamoured;
On bended knee the words of love were stammered;
The blushing schoolgirl blossomed to a bride.
Twenty-five years of happiness have passed,
One lovely daughter symbol of their bliss.
Marriages seldom shine as bright as this:
Love can be brief, but yours was made to last
Eternally. In joy we celebrate
Your silver wedding, blessed by kindly fate.

This entry for the *Observer* limerick competition was published in *Great Green Limericks* (W.H. Allen, 1989).

THE GREENING OF MAGGIE

A blue politician was keen
To join the ecology scene,
So she posed for the press
In a bright yellow dress,
And came out a delicate green.

A competition in a literary weekly in January 1984 called for a verse of potted history.

THE GREATEST MISTAKE

Adolf Hitler looked at Britain;
Feared he might get badly bitten.
When he thought the land was lusher
Sent his armies into Russia.

A reading of Ernest Dowson's fine poem 'Non Sum Qualis Eram' (itself based on Horace's Ode IV.i) inspired these lines in 2002:

THE FADING FLAME

O Venus, spare me now, because
I scarce can play the lover's part,
And I am not the man I was
When good Cynara ruled my heart.

It occurred to me at a local arts festival in 1990 that there was no hymn celebrating the arts in general. I had a possible tune in mind, and this led naturally to the lyric.

HYMN TO THE ARTS

Praise the painters who delight the eye,
Praise the singers raising voices high;
Praise musicians making joyful noise,
Praise the dancers with their grace and poise.
Praise the poets who enrich our hearts,
Praise the actors playing many parts;
Praise the makers of our festival,
And praise the Lord who made them all.

Praise the sculptors carving wood and stone,
Praise composers blending tune and tone;
Praise the novelists whose writing thrills,
Praise the craftsmen for their subtle skills.
Praise the playwrights setting scene on scene,
Praise directors on the stage and screen;
Praise the architects who built our hall,
And praise the Lord who made them all.

During a Caribbean holiday in 1993 I saw hundreds of flying fish, which sometimes landed on the deck of passing vessels. They are considered a great delicacy in the region, and the evening fish markets present a picturesque scene. The words were written on the spot and set to music in 1995.

FLYING FISH

Down in Bridgetown there's a little harbour
Where the fishermen land;
Ev'ry evening you can hear them calling,
With their catch in their hand.

Buy, oh buy me lovely flying fish,
Try, oh try them, they are quite delish;
Fry, oh fry them any way you wish,
My, oh my they're such a tasty dish.

Crowds of people all along the quayside
Come to haggle and buy;
High above all the noisy rumpus
Hear the fishermen cry.

Buy, oh buy me lovely flying fish,
Try, oh try them, they are quite delish;
Fry, oh fry them any way you wish,
My, oh my they're such a tasty dish.

During a National Trust outing I dozed off in the coach and woke up with a melody planted in my mind. It reminded me of the country music I used to hear in Texas in the 1970s, which in turn suggested the subject of the lyric, written in 1995.

QUEEN OF MY HEART

I've lost my dear wife
Who's the love of my life;
She'll always be queen of my heart.

Through good times and bad
She would make me feel glad;
She'll always be queen of my heart.

The day that she died
I just sat down and cried;
I really thought I'd fall apart.

Companion and friend,
She was true to the end;
She'll always be queen of my heart.

This is another lyric that came into my head during a coach trip in 1995. The rhythm required a jaunty verse in the style of contemporary youth – which naturally proved quite a problem! It was set to music later that year.

SEVEN DAYS OF LOVING

We had our honeymoon, we saw the tourist sights,
We loved the sunny days, we loved the starry nights.
I tried to keep in shape like any fitness freak
But baby, seven days of loving make one weak.

We were a loving couple at the loving cup,
We never thought the nectar would be all used up.
Although I used to think I had a strong physique
I know that seven days of loving make one weak.

Oh why is my strength receding
When I'm needing all I've got?
Oh why is my blood congealing
When the feeling should be hot?

You might as well switch off, it isn't any use,
The motor cannot start because it's out of juice.
I'm very sad to say I must have passed my peak
When only seven days of loving make one weak.

Now my head is splitting
I don't mind admitting
Seven days of loving make one weak.

CROSSWORDS

The story behind the first National Crossword Championship in 1970, and the record for the fastest verified solution of the *Times* crossword later that year, based on a lunchtime talk to a Bromley society.

HOW A RECORD WAS SET

Back in London in 1968 after three overseas tours, I settled in a Victorian villa in Bromley, with a commuter journey to London. I started reading *The Times*, and like many other commuters I turned to the back page in the train to try my hand at the crossword. I soon found why it had such a great reputation – the wit of the clues, the wordplay, the double meanings, the hidden anagrams, the literary allusions. Soon I found I could usually complete it, and when the paper announced in June 1970 that they would be running a National Crossword Championship, sponsored by Cutty Sark Whisky, I decided to have a crack at it.

The competition attracted 20,000 solvers and was conducted by post. It started with a straightforward puzzle, followed by a fierce eliminator which narrowed the field to 300. The final was set for a hot weekend in August; as luck would have it, I was on holiday with my family in Ramsgate during the preceding week, and my wife urged me not to travel up to London. But having got so far I thought I might as well continue, so I turned up at the Europa Hotel that Saturday to try my luck.

It turned out to be a marathon, with accuracy and stamina more important than speed. We had to do eight puzzles, being allowed half an hour to complete each one. The top 40 competitors were invited back on Sunday to do four more. To my great astonishment I was declared the winner, with only one error in 376 clues (the dreaded 'Ice-blink'), and averaging 13 minutes on each puzzle. The prize was a silver trophy, a huge bottle of whisky (which I don't drink), and a week for two at the prestigious Carlton Hotel in Cannes.

That was overwhelming enough, but the most unexpected

bonus was the avalanche of publicity. Because the competition was such a novelty, there were reporters and photographers from international press, radio and television, and the event achieved extraordinary coverage throughout the world.

The Times printed my photo on the front page on Monday morning, and in the evening I went to the BBC Television studio to be interviewed by David Dimbleby in the *24 Hours* programme. The next day I was photographed by the *Evening Standard* doing the crossword in the train (a very difficult problem for the cameraman in a crowded commuter compartment!), and the local papers came round for interviews.

I was somewhat taken aback when Tom Driberg wrote a sour comment in his column in the *New Statesman* about my inability to make a coherent statement to the media when receiving the trophy. I discovered later that he was the large bald man competing under the name of 'E. Neill' who had had what I thought was a friendly chat with me when the hubbub died down. Typical of his deviousness, he used to stroll through the magazine's office wearing the bronze Cutty Sark medal (actually given to all 300 finalists), thus giving the impression that he had taken the third prize. He actually finished 198th!

A more pleasant outcome was the batch of letters I received from old friends around the world, some of whom I had lost touch with over the years. And of course the holiday in Cannes, which we took in the following April, was memorable – though it started badly when the hotel management denied any knowledge of us, and the matter had to be sorted out by telex while we waited anxiously in the lobby.

Meanwhile I tried to improve my speed. The journey to Victoria took 23 minutes, and the target was to complete the puzzle by the time the train reached Brixton, then Herne Hill, and so on. One morning in December 1970 I had a few minutes to wait for the train, so with a glance at the station clock I started to do the puzzle on the platform. For once everything clicked, and by the time the train came in the puzzle was completed. I checked the clock and my watch, and was amazed to find I had done it in four and a half minutes.

One of my boys had the *Guinness Book of Records*, and we went through it to see if there was a crossword entry. Oddly enough, while there was a record for the slowest time in doing the *Times* crossword (which was obviously bogus and later removed from the book), there was none for the fastest. I wrote to *The Times* asking if mine might be considered. They published my letter on the Saturday, and at six o'clock that morning I was woken from a deep sleep by a call from BBC Radio 4 saying that they were sending a car to bring me up for an interview on the *Today* programme. I had a shave and a bath and got dressed just as a taxi pulled into the drive, and then we were off in the dark to Broadcasting House. I found myself sharing the billing with a talking dog. I had a chat with Brian Redhead about the crossword, and he then stunned me by pushing *The Times* across and inviting me to set a record by solving that day's puzzle.

Now the Saturday puzzle is a prize one and more difficult than the rest of the week's. My heart sank as he started the stopwatch. But as the crossword editor afterwards explained to me, there had been a mix-up at the printers and the Monday puzzle – the easiest – had been substituted by mistake. It was an enormous stroke of luck, because I was able to run through the puzzle without a pause. When I held my hand up Brian checked his stopwatch and cried: 'I don't believe it – that was three minutes forty-five seconds!' The *Today* team signed the paper to certify the time, and off it went to the *Guinness Book of Records*. The entry appeared in the 1972 edition, and remains to this day – or would do if the editors agreed to reinstate the section on language and literature that they dropped in 1999.

This account of a unique crossword final was published in *Logophile* in 1980.

GOLDEN YEAR FOR A DARK HORSE

The 10th *Times*/Cutty Sark National Crossword Championship took place in 1979 under conditions of unusual difficulty. *The Times* had not been published since November 1978, to the great distress of crossword addicts. With no paper at hand there was no way of communicating with the thousands of fans who would normally take part in the competition.

To their everlasting credit, the Cutty Sark management overcame the problem by advertising in other papers that the competition would still be held and inviting readers to send for the eliminator puzzle. So the first round was conducted entirely through postal channels. Once that was completed, the competition moved into the regional finals stage much as before.

When the national final came along in August there was a top class field. All the previous winners of the competition were among the 16 entrants. There was every indication of a close race, but not much form to go on. The runners were out of practice because they had not been getting their back page exercise. As the television cameras moved around the paddock a good deal of nervousness and sweating could be observed.

We therefore approached the first hurdle with some trepidation. However, I was lucky enough to find it very much to my personal taste. The style of the puzzle was unusual – somewhere between the old *Times* we knew in 1978 and the more difficult *Listener*. Everything fell into place and I had a flying start by completing it in $7^1/_2$ minutes.

When I came out of the 'examination hall' I found I had to wait $5^1/_2$ minutes before my arch rival – the great John Sykes – emerged. I could hardly believe my good fortune that the first puzzle was so much in tune with my temperament. This gave me confidence as we went into the second round.

I certainly needed it, for No. 2 was a real brute. Our genial inquisitor, Edmund Akenhead, always liked to test our mettle with one stiff puzzle, and this was it. I was completely stumped by two interlocking clues at the bottom corner – a little-known romance by Rider Haggard and a concealed quotation from Rupert Brooke.

Who on earth was the 'Haggard but bright-eyed hero (-R--)'? After laboriously running through boys' names I could only come up with Eric and Fred. Fred didn't sound very heroic so I settled for Eric. This gave the outline of C-R-T-S for the 'Grantchester latecomers who left no impression'.

From the shape of the word, and the subject matter of the poem, it had to be 'Curates'. I shoved it in and hoped for the best. I was relieved to see that everyone else was having some kind of trouble (though I discovered afterwards that all of them knew the quotation that had baffled me). I was out in 13 minutes, and felt sure that others would improve on that. Incredibly, when the papers were marked I had moved slightly further ahead of the field, with a lead of 8 minutes.

From then on it was just a matter of keeping my head and not making silly mistakes like leaving out a letter or misspelling a word in the heat of the moment. With the tension easing, I was able to finish the last two in $7^1/_2$ and 6 minutes, to give an average time of $8^1/_2$ minutes for the four puzzles. This was easily my best performance in a final, and totally unexpected.

It was rather embarrassing for the BBC-TV team who had filmed all the well-known competitors before the race and were waiting to slot in the name of the winner in the 5.50 news. They had to say that the final had been won by a dark horse!

Ironically the final of the 1979 competition probably received more publicity than any in recent years. The story went out through the international wire services and cropped up all over the world. It even featured in a long and absorbing account in the *New Yorker* of the shut-down at *The Times*. A particularly happy outcome for me was that the news brought me into touch with many old friends in Britain and abroad.

A musical tribute to a master composer and puzzle buff.

MUSIC IN THE SQUARE

A square of eight letters can be filled in from the following clues:

1. Admonishes as this chap composes... (8).
2. ...a musical drama (8).
3. The Lily of Lagoon-a? (8).
4. An instrument within one's hearing (4).
   What chart-toppers do best (4).
5. 'Roses of Picardy' would bear them (4).
   Song from *The King and I* inserted in *Carmen* (4).
6. Webster's producing *La Scala di Seta* (8).
7. Puccini, Verdi, etc. (8).
8. It helps to achieve perfect pitch (4).
   A recess for the choir (4).

[Solution on page 230]

This anecdote was published in the *Reader's Digest* in November 1984. It is used slightly differently in Colin Dexter's masterpiece *The Remorseful Day.*

CLUED UP

During a Transatlantic flight I was engrossed in a crossword puzzle and did not hear the announcement that we were approaching land. My stewardess leaned over and said: 'Your next clue is "Truss neatly to be safe (6,4,4,5)".'

I was quite baffled until I realised that she had given me a perfect anagram of 'Fasten your seat belts'.

An address when making a presentation to the retiring crossword editor at the final of the Collins Dictionaries/*Times* National Crossword Championship in September 1983.

HOMAGE TO THE HEADMASTER

My mind goes back to a warm Sunday afternoon in August 1970, when we had just completed a marathon two-day session of twelve puzzles in the first Cutty Sark/*Times* national crossword championship. We were then introduced to our chief inquisitor, Edmund Akenhead. I suppose few of us until that day realised that *The Times* had a crossword editor.

When we met this impressive combination of judge and headmaster we were somewhat overawed. It is true that in subsequent years some bold spirits in the regional and national finals have had the temerity to propose alternative solutions. I count myself very fortunate to have squeezed past the magisterial eye in 1979 with an unusual spelling of 'dietitian'. But once the familiar brown suitcase has been opened and the reference books have been consulted, few have sought to question the master's judgments.

But, of course, the annual competition that brings us so pleasantly together is only the tip of the iceberg. Each year we are offered over 300 puzzles. I see that yesterday we reached No. 16,225. Ronald and Jane Carton, in their editorships between 1930 and 1965, laid the foundations of a reputation that has spread worldwide. One has only to think of the novels, plays and films in which characters are pictured battling with the *Times* crossword to realise what a national institution it has become. All credit to those who set the standard.

Then in 1965 there arrived the man who has subtly improved and refined the *Times* crossword into a form of literary art. He has imposed his personal stamp on it. He has encouraged his team of compilers to develop qualities of verbal dexterity, of wit, of fairness, of intelligence, of all-round excellence, that have kept us enthralled for 18 years. If the standard of the *Times had* been out of joint, then surely he would have been born to set it right. I think we can say that he has done us great service, and we have all thrived under his tutelage.

And we must never forget the Jumbos which first confronted us in 1970. What elephantine elegance, what breadth of erudition – what excitement as the solver is led on from Shakespeare to Shaw, from Bible to Brewer, from Ancient Greece to modern science, until the onset of writer's cramp forces the pen from his fingers. How fitting that the name of Akenhead could be clued as 'a knowledge master'.

But Edmund Akenhead is more than the master who sets us our daily task. I think it true to say that, since he has become publicly visible, he has come to be regarded by many of us as a personal friend. This must be a unique experience – for a literary editor on a daily newspaper to have such a bond with his readers.

Some years ago I had the privilege of meeting Earl Attlee when he came to Colombo as the guest of the Government of Ceylon. As the junior member of the British High Commission I was appointed his official contact. I called on him at his hotel and asked if he needed anything. In his laconic way he said: '*The Times* – cricket and crossword'. I was able to let him have our airmail edition, only one day late, and he settled down happily with his pipe and pen. His two interests are perfectly compatible.

Francis Thompson celebrated the run-stealers in his immortal line:

'O my Hornby and my Barlow long ago'.

I should like to think that, in years to come, some poet will write of the crossword with equal felicity and – perhaps mindful of the tortures that his brain had suffered at the hands of the master – end his ode with the words:

'O my Akenhead in London long ago'.

This tribute to Dr John Sykes – translator, lexicographer, theoretical physicist and brilliant crossword solver – was given at the final of the *Times*/Knockando National Crossword Championship on 12 September 1993.

THE GREATEST SOLVER

John Sykes (1929–1993)

I was saddened to read the news of John Sykes' death in *The Times* last week. Like many of you, I had the greatest admiration for his linguistic prowess and speed of thought which led him to ten victories in these annual championships.

At times we amateurs might have grumbled about having to pit our puny wits against a professional lexicographer – and there was no doubt that what he himself called a 'marginal advantage' put him head and shoulders above the rest of us. I am reminded of the description of Julius Caesar which Shakespeare almost wrote:

> Why man, he doth bestride the chequered grid
> Like a colossus, and we petty men
> Walk under his huge legs, and peep about
> To find ourselves perpetual runners-up.

I'm sure that we fellow competitors approached the finals with some trepidation. You might even say, in modern parlance, that we were 'psyched' out. At the top of his form John was unstoppable. In 1974 he completed the four puzzles in 29 minutes, with a record margin of $12\frac{1}{2}$ minutes over his nearest rival. This means that he would have solved five puzzles in the time we took to do four.

However, he was the first to admit that he was not infallible, having lost to James Atkins in 1971 through omitting a letter. I was fortunate enough to beat him by six minutes in 1979, when he was clearly unwell, but he walloped me the following year. He also lost to Bill Pilkington in 1987 and 1988, but came back strongly to regain the title in 1989.

153

Unlike mine, his mental powers did not seem to deteriorate with age. In the 1989 final he averaged $7^1/_2$ minutes, and at his last appearance in 1990 his average time was eight minutes. It was a tragedy that ill health prevented him from continuing.

At first sight John gave the impression of an ascetic character, a dry old stick. The fruits of his crossword success held little interest for him. In the early days he gave away foreign holidays to friends, and giant bottles of whisky to charity raffles. He was certainly a very private person. But on closer acquaintance he revealed a nice sense of humour, and I recall flashes of erudite wit when he addressed us after his victories.

John was essentially a *Times* crossword man. He didn't care for the *Listener* or Azed puzzles, which he found 'too convoluted'. But strangely enough, he wasn't a *Times* reader. So how did he perfect his expertise on the crossword? Well, it was reported that a friend used to give him a weekly batch of puzzles, and that he sat down and solved them all at once. He had hit on the ideal training for our annual competitions!

As we know from his outstanding achievements in various careers, as well documented in the *Times* obituary, John was a polymath, a man of brilliant intellect. Not many of us will have known him in his professional capacity, though, so our memories of him are mostly restricted to his crossword feats. In this field he was pre-eminent. That being so, it was generous of him to stand down in alternate years to give the others a chance.

His keen analytical mind went straight to the nub of the clue, however much the setter tried to disguise it, and his general knowledge was so all-embracing that no subject could baffle him. I should like to salute John Sykes as the greatest solver of our *Times*.

A contribution to the British Council's touring exhibition on 'Wordplay' in 1993.

THE CULT OF THE CROSSWORD

What is the world's favourite intellectual pastime – is it chess, bridge, mah jongg, backgammon, Scrabble? No, it's none of these – it's solving crossword puzzles.

The crossword puzzle is one of the most universally popular inventions of the twentieth century. In Britain alone, several million people enjoy their daily dose of puzzling. It's estimated that over 80 per cent of the world's daily newspapers carry some form of crossword, as well as many weekly papers and magazines.

The crossword appears to be a combination of the old acrostics and word squares which date back to ancient Greece. The first one was devised in 1913 by Arthur Wynne, an English journalist working on the New York *Sunday World*. Looking to provide his readers with some entertainment, he composed a diamond-shaped grid with all the words interlocking and simple definition clues. He called it a 'Word-cross'.

But it wasn't until April 1924, with the publication by Simon & Shuster of the first crossword puzzle book, that the craze took off. It immediately swept America and dominated social life. It got so bad that dictionaries had to be provided on trains so that commuters could do their puzzles.

A scornful editorial in the London *Times* in December 1924 noted that 'All America has succumbed to the crossword puzzle... The crossword is a menace because it is making devastating inroads on the working hours of every rank of society'. But two months later *The Times* had to admit that 'the craze had crossed the Atlantic with the speed of a meteorological depression'.

The Times itself held out as long as it could, but in the end it bowed to public pressure and published its first crossword on 1 February 1930. It was one of the first daily papers to move away from the simple definition type of clue and introduce the 'cryptic' clue which has to be unravelled before the solver can arrive at the answer. Its diamond jubilee in 1990 was marked with great celebrations and worldwide coverage.

Though not the hardest of its kind, its consistent qualities of sophisticated wordplay and sly humour have won it a reputation as the most famous crossword in the world. It frequently features in novels, plays and films where the author wishes to establish a character of high intelligence. The annual *Times* National Crossword Championship, which has been held since 1970, attracts up to 20,000 entrants, and the final is a most exciting event as the keenest minds in the country work through four puzzles against the clock.

Why should the cryptic crossword have developed only in Britain? One answer is the Englishman's fondness for wordplay. The 1920s were a period when the country house party was at its height, and it was customary for people to settle down to charades and pencil-and-paper games after dinner. Edward Powys Mathers, a critic, poet and translator, picked up this tradition and translated it into the crossword, calling himself Torquemada after the Grand Inquisitor.

Secondly, the English language has evolved over time as a melting-pot of words derived from many sources. In addition to the Romance and North European languages which form the basis of the English tongue, there are words brought back by Britons from the former colonies, infusions from Chinese and Russian, contributions from Turkish and Arabic. Greek provides the basis of political thought, science and technology, Latin for religion, medicine and the arts.

English has eagerly taken in everything. Consequently the language contains many words with multiple meanings, deriving from completely different roots. Even short words like 'set' can have a hundred different meanings. And it is not uncommon for a single word like 'round' to serve as noun, verb, adverb, adjective and preposition. These ambiguities are seized upon by crafty crossword compilers who manipulate the language to their own ends to confuse and mislead the solver.

Thirdly, the English language is unique in possessing so many short words which can be used to make up longer ones to which they are in no way related. Take the word 'insignificant' for example. It breaks down neatly into 'in-sign-if-I-can't'. Or 'refrigerator', which becomes 'ref-rig-era-tor'. Tricks of this kind are the meat and drink of crossword compilers. With the most sophisticated practitioners of this form of literary fun, 'brainwash' may be broken down as 'bra-in-wash' and clued as 'Bust down reason'.

Anagrams are no longer indicated by the symbol 'anag' in brackets, but by words in the clue suggesting confusion, error, drunkenness, building, possibility and so on. Thus, 'The President *saw nothing* wrong' may be construed as 'Washington'. Taking this to its highest form, the whole clue becomes a definition of the answer, as in ' *Thing called* shaky illumination?', giving 'candlelight'.

Then there are many instances of one word slipped inside another to make a third, as in 'ca(bare)t', 'come(lines)s' and 'th(ink)ing . Sometimes a word is hidden; for example, 'Prime Minister seen in the Athenaeum' gives 'Heath'.

Another popular device is words that sound alike: 'wether', 'weather' and 'whether' are typical of this kind. In some cases a foreign import can sound like an English word: the rubber substance 'gutta-percha' becomes the street urchin 'gutter-percher'.

The crossword compiler has all these tricks up his sleeve, and many more. His tool is the English language in its infinite flexibility, and he uses it to baffle the solver in a devious but entertaining fashion. If you are looking for mental stimulation – and an excellent way of enlarging your vocabulary – why not try an English cryptic crossword?

The editor of the *Guinness Book of Records* invited the champions to contribute any unusual incidents arising from their entries in the book. An abridged version of this account appeared in the 1995 edition.

CROSSWORD DIPLOMACY

During my career in the Diplomatic Service I always found that cultural diplomacy played an important role in getting to know people of influence and opening the way to promoting HMG's policies, as well as British goods and services. In various countries I was invited by press, radio and TV to give my views on matters of current interest, and made many public speeches. I opened art exhibitions and a Shakespeare festival, and judged a beauty competition. In this context it was enormously helpful that, by a great stroke of good fortune, I happened to hold the world record for the fastest solution of the *Times* crossword.

A curious episode stemming from this came about in 1976. At that time I was on the FCO desk handling our economic relations with the Indian subcontinent, and had done some research into the figures of our exports to those countries. Analysis showed that our trade with India was not flourishing as well as it should, given the close historic and commercial links between the two countries and the size of our bilateral aid programme.

Following talks with Indian officials it was agreed that trade relations would benefit from the formal framework of a bilateral economic cooperation agreement. The terms were drawn up, and I travelled to New Delhi with Peter Shore, the Secretary of State for Trade, for the official signing of the agreement (which incidentally has proved very beneficial to both sides).

We were cordially received and entertained by our Indian counterparts. The Indian Government and people had never forgotten that it was a Labour Government in Britain in 1947 that had granted India independence with a parliamentary system of government – the largest democracy in the world. There was an instinctive bond between the Congress Party of India and the British Labour Party.

But it was some time since a British Cabinet Minister had paid an official visit to New Delhi, and naturally Mr Shore wished to call on Mrs Indira Gandhi and discuss India's progress. However, there was a problem of protocol. It became clear that whereas the Indian Prime Minister would have been glad to meet her British opposite number officially, in accordance with strict protocol she would not be able to see a mere trade minister.

I discussed the problem with her private secretary, an old friend from his days at the Indian High Commission in London, when we found we shared a common interest in E.M. Forster. He knew that Mrs Gandhi liked to do a cryptic crossword, and mentioned to her that I was the *Times* champion. Incredibly, for one so preoccupied with affairs of state, she agreed to see me.

Thus it came about that I was ushered into her sanctum for a chat about our shared enthusiasm, with the Minister waiting in the wings. She told me she liked to relax with a crossword at the end of the day, while I preferred to tackle one early in the morning to clear my mind. I was privileged to have a most interesting conversation with Mrs Gandhi for ten minutes.

As I thanked her for her kindness, I asked if she would like to meet Mr Shore, who was in the room next door. 'Of course', she replied. The ice having been broken, the Minister was invited to pay a courtesy call on her. He was able to conduct his official business in a very useful meeting which helped to reinforce UK–India relations at the highest level.

Another piece of crossword diplomacy occurred some years later in a sporting fixture.

PEN VERSUS PUNCH

At the end of my career in the Diplomatic Service, when I was Acting British High Commissioner to Ghana, an enterprising lady journalist on the *Mirror*, the leading local newspaper, spotted that I was in the *Guinness Book of Records* as a world crossword champion, together with Azumah Nelson, the Ghanaian world featherweight boxing champion. She arranged for us to meet in November 1986 at the Accra Stadium, where Azumah was in training for the next defence of his title.

I showed him a sample of the *Times* crossword, and he asked what my record was. When I told him it was 3 minutes 45 seconds he thought the time was pretty good, but went on to say he had done even better because in 1985 he had knocked out a challenger in the first round in 2 minutes 24 seconds. We agreed that Azumah had won on points.

This unusual encounter was reported in the *Mirror* with a splendid photograph showing paper and pen versus boxing gloves. A week later, on a Saturday morning, an official from the Foreign Ministry called at my residence and told me I was summoned to the Castle – the seat of Government. To the head of a diplomatic mission, such a summons often means bad news – for example, that the Government to which he is accredited is to make a protest – and I was prepared for the worst.

Imagine my surprise when I was ushered into the presence of the Head of State, Jerry Rawlings, who had been Chairman of the Provisional National Defence Council (PNDC) since 1981. He was accompanied by the Chief Secretary (the equivalent of Prime Minister).

They greeted me warmly, and mentioned that they had seen the newspaper report. They were impressed by my appearance in the record book, which they took to be a sign of high intelligence. I was completely unprepared by what followed. Rawlings went on to ask whether I could offer any advice on how his government might improve the lot of the people of Ghana. What on earth could I say in that situation, coming out of the blue?

I racked my brains (much as I would have done with a problem in a crossword) and ventured a few off-the-cuff comments. I pointed out that some foreign publications still mistakenly referred to his regime as a 'military government', being ignorant of the real situation in Ghana. Some countries even had difficulties about their relationship with a non-elected government that appeared undemocratic. This had some serious consequences – such as the unwillingness of several prominent donor countries to provide aid to Ghana because their constitutions forbade it. Elections would legitimise his government in the eyes of the international community.

I said that the British Government had been watching with great pleasure Ghana's economic progress under his leadership – and had indeed contributed materially to that progress. I added that Rawlings was a popular, charismatic leader and had a first-rate team of technocrats running his Ministries. If he went to the country he could be certain of being elected President with his capable government more or less intact – but with the added advantage of winning financial support from new quarters abroad. He nodded thoughtfully, as was his wont, thanked me, and we parted on the friendliest of terms. I left Ghana shortly afterwards, on my retirement from the Diplomatic Service, but naturally continued to follow events there.

In 1992 I was intrigued by the announcement that elections would be held in Ghana, and pleased when Jerry Rawlings was elected President. He was re-elected in 1996 and served out another full term under the new constitution. HM the Queen paid a highly successful State Visit to Ghana in November 1999, and President Rawlings was invited to Britain in 2000 before he retired from public office at the beginning of 2001.

CRYPTIC CROSSWORD CLUES

Word-building, anagrams and double meanings are central to these clues. The *Chambers Dictionary* (1998) is recommended.

1. They convey one through the heights (8).

2. Courtiers heard building fences (9).

3. Important instruction to assistant by outgoing dictator (11).

4. Writer who scandalised the educational Establishment (8).

5. You'll find drunken ravers in any celebration (11).

6. Two chaps, mature fellows, start to tackle staff organisation (3-10).

7. Does cad love it? You can bet it! (5,4).

8. Carsmiths out on strike for holiday bonus (9,3).

9. Judge has to fix period to run in the cooler (12).

10. Woman ensnaring endless men, rich (5,6).

11. Alight from the old Peruvian line (12).

12. 'E' could spell death for a girl (8,6).

13. Thing called shaky illumination (11).

14. Composer is hardly in debt to the audience (7).

15. Problem (non-religious) recurring in Hibernian writer (4,7).

16. Novelist depicting car-crazy university (4,5,4).

17. It envelops the family in choking fumes (7).

18. Firm not making a profit? (10).

19. Last-minute recovery gives result to the side (9).

20. What models do suited Titian wonderfully (12).

21. A nit is often the product of this (11).

22. She gets to practise on her dancing (13).

23. Where you might see nude in improper act? (7).

24. Awful relations whom nothing will keep away (7-2-3).

25. Long one characteristic of cats? (8).

26. Dive from height into waters unknown (9).

27. Feature of a posh address in Groombridge? (8-4).

28. Fighter crew here – then and now! (7).

29. This player takes the hole in one (6).

30. Losing one's head – like Philip II losing his (9).

31. Ex-President of the Glove Commission (10).

32. If one cold foot is numb, two must be (4,6).

33. Run commercial vehicles and time the speed (12).

34. Old ruler warns what conspirators are (2,7).

35. Source of laughter among rustics? (10).

36. He investigates what turns persons to crime (9,5).

37. Herb admits Earl's transformed as a composer (6,4).

38. Likeness must be good to capture men with character (11).

39. Part of the State Carriages in use at Sandringham? (6,3).

40. Mavis' shorts hung crookedly (4,6).

41. Ducks scattered by shotgun (7).

42. Beer in St Tropez running out? Heads for the bar! (6).

43. Canvassed main views (9).

44. For excavation further north, wanderer returned (8,3).

45. Disadvantages of a public school (8).

46. Time to celebrate in the wildest way ever seen (3,5,3).

47. Two jobs in the public service (4,6).

48. Situation, say, when embraced by boyfriend (3-4).

49. Gunfire recently heard? Get the smelling salts! (3,8).

50. In which high dangler somehow loses height? (4-6).

[Solutions on page 232]

LYRIC-WRITERS

An article published in *Words & Music* in 1989.

THE POETRY OF POPULAR SONG

I grew up with the popular music of the 1930s, when radio was the main medium of entertainment for the average family. By listening carefully to the radio you could pick up the words of the songs. The pattern of the lyric owed something to the familiar hymns of the 18th and 19th centuries. There was a standard form of composition of 64 measures, which gave the lyric-writer 16 lines; these usually broke down into four verses running A-A-B-A. The lyrics were often well written; they rhymed neatly, told a story, described a situation, or just made a statement about the person's feelings.

Many of these songs are still being sung today – 70 years on. They have survived because the words are as well remembered as the tunes. But whereas the composers of the music (and the singers and the bands) have been duly recognised and are well known to the general public, few people would have heard of the authors of the lyrics. Their names are seldom mentioned by programme presenters – and this in itself seems odd, given that the author not only writes the lyric but more often than not is responsible for the title of the song.

There are, of course, major exceptions. Numerous radio and television programmes, films and books have been devoted to the lives and works of the acknowledged masters of the lyric, who might be termed the First Eleven: Cole Porter, Irving Berlin and Noël Coward (who also wrote their own music), Ira Gershwin, Lorenz Hart, Oscar Hammerstein II, Howard Dietz, Dorothy Fields, Yip Harburg, Johnny Mercer and Frank Loesser (who later became his own composer). Their work between the two World Wars was of such high quality that their names have lived on.

But what of the lesser-known lyricists who contributed so much to the golden age of popular song, and have never received proper recognition through books, films, radio or

167

television? Writers like Herman Hupfeld, author of 'As Time Goes By', who doesn't even figure in the credits of the film *Casablanca*, which relied so heavily on his splendid and enduring song? And Otto Harbach ('Smoke Gets in Your Eyes'), Mitchell Parish ('Star Dust'), Leo Robin ('Thanks for the Memory'), and Irving Caesar ('Tea for Two').

I thought it was high time to pay tribute to these neglected lyricists. The obvious medium was radio, but where to begin? Since these writers were virtually unknown it was difficult to track down any detailed information about them in the standard reference works on Broadway shows, Hollywood musicals and Tin Pan Alley. It was a question of gleaning the occasional snippet of background about the lyrics that could be indexed against each writer. Record sleeves were sometimes helpful, while songbooks provided the lyrics to be analysed. The American Society of Composers, Authors & Publishers (ASCAP) was extremely cooperative in supplying useful biographical data.

Gradually the idea took shape of a series of 12 radio programmes called *The Poetry of Popular Song*. The format of each programme would be a brief biographical sketch; any available anecdotes or reminiscences; some contemporary recordings illustrating the writer's work; some discussion of his distinctive style and special achievements; and an attempt to place him in the popular music scene of the period.

This proposal was accepted by Radio 4, but with the proviso that each programme would be limited to 15 minutes. Timing was therefore of the essence, as each lyric had to be dovetailed into the narrative. The BBC Gramophone Library provided facilities for me to play LP records (this was in the days before CDs took over the market) and to select the versions I needed.

And then I had one great stroke of luck. Mitch Parish was then very old and in poor health, but he agreed to give an interview in his New York apartment that produced a mine of priceless stories about himself and his contemporaries. This tape supplied live material to brighten up the broadcasts.

Three series of four programmes each were broadcast

between 1989 and 1991. Reviews were generally favourable, and the audience response very encouraging. There were unexpected windfalls. For example, Otto Harbach's daughter-in-law picked up the programme on him in North Africa, and was delighted to hear the tribute to his genius. An old colleague I had lost touch with many years ago heard the broadcast and returned two books he had borrowed in 1951! And an ingenious cryptic crossword in the *Listener* was based on the series.

The research also provided enough information for articles on several members of my lyrical team, published in *The Times* and music journals. These are printed in the following pages.

This article was published in *Words & Music* in November 2000.

LAUREATE OF THE STARRY SKIES

Early in 2000 a TV viewers' poll on BBC2 nominated the ten best song lyrics of the 20th century. Remarkably, only one came from the golden age of popular music between the wars: 'Stardust'. Even then, the presenters attributed it to the composer rather than the lyric-writer!

'Stardust', written over 70 years ago, is the most recorded popular song of all time, and one of the most perfect. I suppose everyone knows that Hoagy Carmichael composed the music, and very fine it is, but the leisurely, contemplative lyric has an excellence of its own. It was written by Mitchell Parish (1900–1993), deservedly known as the 'Poet Laureate of Tin Pan Alley', but largely neglected by the reference books.

When I interviewed him in his New York apartment in 1988 for my Radio 4 series on *The Poetry of Popular Song*, he was in very poor health but still eloquent and witty as befitted a Phi Beta Kappa English graduate of Columbia University. He had marvellous powers of recall about the early days of his songwriting career, describing vividly how he served his apprenticeship with Mills Music as a young song plugger working with vaudeville singers like Sophie Tucker and Eddie Cantor. On a salary of 12 dollars a week from his publishing house he used to go backstage and try and get them to sing its songs. His big breakthrough as a lyricist came in 1929 with 'Stardust'. He explained how the song came about.

'Hoagy Carmichael was on the staff, getting a weekly stipend because he was composing music for Jack Mills' publishing firm. They came to me with a tune that Hoagy had written. It was a swing tune, and it went something like this: di-da-di-da-da-da-da-da-di-da-di-da. I didn't see anything special about it so I didn't write the lyric. But subsequently Victor Young arranged this tune. Now it was entirely different, and that is the way the song is today – romantic, smooth, a beautiful mellow melody. When I heard that tune, I wrote the lyric'.

The Mills Music company specialised in transforming jazz instrumentals into mainstream popular songs by adding a lyric, and Parish was their star performer because his lyrics frequently effected this kind of transformation with great versatility. For example, while he used poetic imagery and high-flown language for 'Stardust', he adopted a more vernacular style in 1928 for 'Sweet Lorraine', a composition by Cliff Burwell that has always been a favourite with jazz players.

There is one marvellous song for which Mitchell Parish wrote the lyric but is not given the credit. His boss Jack Mills had the sneaky habit of getting his own name printed on the sheet music as if he had made a major contribution to the song. So it happened that 'Mood Indigo', usually attributed to Duke Ellington but actually composed by his clarinettist Barney Bigard, was published in 1931 with Mills as the lyricist. It's a melancholy lament, in conversational phrasing, with the insistent sounds of Oo and Oh to match the blue mood.

Parish enjoyed the challenge of writing lyrics for tunes that were unorthodox in their construction, away from the usual 32-bar format. 'Sophisticated Lady' is another fascinating example of his talent for the unusual. This started as an instrumental piece composed by Duke Ellington and frequently played by his band. The convoluted melody calls for a very complex verse form which Parish handles brilliantly, working in a superb sequence of rhymes: 'nonchalant', 'restaurant' and 'what you want'. Truly a most sophisticated lyric for the lady concerned.

In 1934 Parish responded to Hoagy Carmichael's music again for a nice song called 'One Morning in May', writing a very romantic lyric with some clever internal rhymes. Peggy Lee, a great fan of Parish's work, may have had this in mind when she described 'the pleasurable emotions a singer feels when the words shine and one sees pictures and the rhymes roll around on the tongue like Belgian chocolate'.

171

Parish returned to his favourite celestial theme in 1934 with 'Stars Fell on Alabama', to music by Frank Perkins. I'd always been intrigued by this odd preoccupation with heavenly bodies that seemed to run throughout his song lyrics. Was this just a coincidence or was there a reason why? His response was illuminating.

'First of all, I want to go on record that I am not a vampire, a nocturnal creature! Seriously speaking, I admit that I've written many songs that deal with moonlight and stars. Originally I came from down south in America, in the state of Louisiana. When I came up north, I was about three years old and my parents settled in the Lower East Side of New York, which is probably equivalent to the East End of London. I would say that the people who resided in that area were not affluent.

'We lived in tenements and at night you very rarely saw the stars. I'm not trying to psychoanalyse my background, why I wrote the songs dealing with stars and moonlight, but perhaps it was the fact that I didn't see too many stars at night and I didn't see moonlight. It may be an escape from my environment, my longing for stars and moonlight, and it probably expressed itself in my songwriting.'

Parish had his greatest astronomical year in 1939, starting with 'Stairway to the Stars'. This was taken from a theme in *Park Avenue Fantasy*, a concerto by Matt Malneck and Frank Signorella, violinist and pianist respectively in Paul Whiteman's Orchestra. Parish's lyric made it a smash hit.

We have only to hear the first sustained note of Glenn Miller's signature tune to know that we're listening to his own composition, 'Moonlight Serenade'. It began as an instrumental piece orchestrated in his unique style, which is the one we know better than the vocal arrangement, with the atmospheric lyric added by Mitchell Parish.

The year ended with 'Deep Purple'. Parish explained that it was originally one of the themes of a concert piece by Peter DeRose composed in 1934 for the Paul Whiteman Orchestra. Parish was so impressed by the music that he took two strains from it and made two songs: 'Lilacs in the Rain' and 'Deep

Purple'. There's a lovely evocative picture in the opening lines
of the latter:

> When the deep purple falls
> Over sleepy garden walls.
> And the stars begin to flicker in the sky.

Parish is unique as a lyricist in that he hardly ever worked in
direct collaboration with a composer. Most of his lyrics were
written some time after the melody was composed. But what
makes him so distinguished a writer is that his lyrics always
fit perfectly with the melody, and in every case the song
became a greater hit when his words were added.

Parish described himself as an unashamed romantic, and
this aspect of his personality comes out strongly in his lyrics.
He published a book of verse called *For Those in Love,* and
he contributed sonnets to Walter Winchell's widely syndi-
cated newspaper column. But ever versatile, he also wrote
lyrics for novelty, swing and rhythm songs like 'Organ
Grinder's Swing' and produced lively translations of foreign
hits such as 'Volare', by the Italian composer Domenico
Modugno.

After retiring as a lyricist Mitchell Parish built up quite a
reputation as a lecturer on songwriting and the musical
theatre. The final accolade came in 1987 with a Broadway
show celebrating 34 of his songs. Naturally it was called
Stardust. That's the song he will always be remembered for –
the mellow masterpiece of his youth, the melody which will
remain the memory of love's refrain.

This tribute to a neglected songwriter was published in *The Times* in January 1994 to mark the centenary of his birth.

THE NOBODY BEHIND A SONG IN A MILLION

Born 100 years ago, Herman Hupfeld left an indelible
mark on popular music – 'As Time Goes By'

'Play it once, Sam, for old time's sake'.
'Ah don't know what you mean, Miss Ilsa'.
'Play it, Sam. Play "As Time Goes By"'.

Ingrid Bergman's request – indeed, large chunks of dialogue from *Casablanca* – will be familiar to millions throughout the world. The words Dooley Wilson is persuaded to sing are among the most-quoted of all time. Yet Herman Hupfeld, the song's writer, remains virtually unknown.

His name does not appear in the film credits, where the music arranger, Max Steiner (who didn't even like the song) is given the honours. He's not credited in *As Time Goes By*, Laurence Leaner's biography of Bergman, or in the current television sitcom of that name. Only Alan Jay Lerner, in his celebration of *The Musical Theatre*, gives Hupfeld full credit for his masterpiece.

The song was actually written for Frances Williams to sing in the Broadway revue *Everybody's Welcome*, which opened at the Shubert Theatre on 14 October 1931. Not that it caused a great stir at the time, and the show was soon forgotten. But the song remained in people's minds through the affection of night club pianists and singers like Elisabeth Welch. And it finally came into its own 11 years later in the Hollywood film, where its lush orchestration dominated the soundtrack.

Just about everyone knows 'As Time Goes By' from the film: the powerful and painful associations it carries for Bergman and Bogart, the surging melody, the phrases that have become part of the language. But not so well known is the clever introductory verse, rarely sung, describing the pressures of change and the uncertainties of modern life, before the lyric launches into the famous chorus.

Little is known about Hupfeld's life. He was born in Montclair, a small town to the north-west of New York, on 1 February 1894. He must have been something of a musical prodigy, for when nine years old he was sent to Germany to study the violin. Returning to America, he was educated at the local high school. But he was soon bitten by the show business bug, and at 18 he played and sang his own songs in *Ziegfeld's Midnight Frolic*.

After service in the US Navy in the First World War, Hupfeld continued his career as a pianist and entertainer. He started writing witty songs for the fashionable Broadway revues, including the *Little Shows* at the Music Box Theatre. 'Sing Something Simple' (1930) and 'When Yuba Plays the Rumba on the Tuba' (1931) were two of his numbers from these revues.

Typical of his light-hearted style is a song that is often played nowadays on the soundtrack to documentaries about the Depression years: 'Let's Put Out the Lights and Go to Sleep', from *Music Hall Varieties* in 1932. Not for Hupfeld the stark social realism of Yip Harburg's 'Brother Can You Spare a Dime', which appeared only the month before, but the wrily humorous resignation of a young couple surveying the scene after a hectic party, summed up in the line: 'What's to do about it?'

Despite the sophistication of his songs, Hupfeld doesn't seem to have been a very outgoing character. Mitch Parish, who wrote the lyrics to the classic 'Stardust' in 1929, told me he once met Hupfeld standing on his own at a convention of the American Society of Authors, Composers and Publishers in the late 1920s. Parish, just starting out as a lyricist, approached Hupfeld (who had written no hits at that time) and asked whether he would like to collaborate on a song. He was given a cool brush-off, Hupfeld stating rather stuffily that he always wrote his own lyrics.

During the Second World War Hupfeld travelled widely, entertaining the troops at camps and hospitals in America and Europe. He died in his home town on 8 June 1951. It seems like a quiet and uneventful life, a far cry from the lives of many of his contemporaries on the popular music scene.

One reason for Hupfeld's relative obscurity is that he never composed the full score for a Broadway show or a Hollywood musical. He was essentially a miniature artist, writing songs that were interpolated into other people's revues.

But Hupfeld surely deserves to be remembered for that one classic piece in which the romantic lyric perfectly matches the brooding melody, a song whose magic continues to enchant us as time goes by.

This article, originally written for Irving Caesar's centenary in 1995, was published in *Words & Music* in March 2001.

SONGWRITER'S TEATIME TRIUMPH

How Caesar adopted a British custom

The phrase 'tea for two' sounds quintessentially English; and the song of that name has come to symbolise the bright young things of the Twenties. But it couldn't be more American in origin. Its New York author, Irving Caesar, who celebrated his hundredth birthday in 1995 (appropriately on 4 July), was the oldest surviving lyric-writer from the golden age of popular song.

Caesar once recalled how he came to write the lyric while revising the score of *No, No, Nanette* with composer Vincent Youmans for the Chicago try-out in 1924. 'One day I took a late nap in my apartment. Youmans came by to wake me up to take me to a party. As I was dressing, he said: "Something came to me this morning", and he sat down to play it.

'Youmans asked me for a lyric but I reminded him of the party. Still he insisted. I said: "I'll write a dummy lyric and do the real one in the morning". In a little more than five minutes the words came to me. That lyric, though it was supposed to be only temporary, was never changed.'

His instant response is all the more remarkable given the relentless, metronomic regularity of Youmans' music, leaving the lyricist to cope with a succession of very short lines. But Caesar realised that he could enhance the hypnotic effect of the tune by fitting a simple rhyme scheme into consecutive bars – you, knee, two, tea – stepping up to five rhymes in the second verse – break, awake, bake, cake, take – and closing with five more – family, me, see, we, be. Simplicity can sometimes be more effective than sophistication.

The song is not about tea-drinking, of course, but about a young couple who just want to enjoy their own company. In

177

1925 it became the smash hit of the show in London and on Broadway, and a huge success all over the world – partly because the title translates easily into many languages. Shostakovich was so taken with the tune that he made an amusing arrangement of it as 'Tahiti Trot'.

Caesar was official stenographer for the Henry Ford Peace Ship in the First World War, and then worked as a mechanic in the Ford plant. But his heart was set on show business. As a young man he had spent his spare time going round the music publishers of Tin Pan Alley, trying to sell his lyrics. He often stopped off at Remick's to hear his old schoolmate, George Gershwin, play the piano. When Gershwin got a job as rehearsal pianist for the Broadway show, *Miss 1917*, he had a chance to play some of his own songs, and Caesar supplied the words. That launched his career as a lyricist.

In 1919 the opening of a new movie theatre was to be celebrated by a revue. Gershwin and Caesar contributed a song that took shape as they rode home on the top of a bus. They called it 'Swanee'. Al Jolson liked the song and it became a hit in his current Broadway show, *Sinbad*. It sold over a million copies of sheet music and two million records, making $10,000 apiece for composer and author. Surprisingly, in view of his later masterpieces, it was Gershwin's best-selling song.

Caesar collaborated with a number of other composers as well as Youmans. His 'Crazy Rhythm' (1928) matched the short repeated fragments of the music to suggest a nervous lover, while 'Animal Crackers in My Soup' (1935), a charming little number devised for Shirley Temple, became her favourite song. He had another smash hit in 1936 with 'Is It True What They Say About Dixie?', written at high speed for Al Jolson's radio show.

He became a music publisher in New York, and when well into his eighties he still went every day to his office on Seventh Avenue, smoking his habitual big cigar. Naturally he became much in demand as a shrewd commentator on songs and songwriting. Some years ago he summed up his profession with these words:

'The popular song of the past half-century had the largest impact on American culture of any so-called art form. Why, for God's sake, the popular song *is* American culture'.

Caesar once told an audience, at the risk of sounding a little immodest, that most of his songs were written in less than 15 minutes. He was also noted for his quick wit. When asked: 'Which comes first, the words or the music?' he replied: 'What comes first is the contract!'

(Irving Caesar died on 17 December 1996, aged 101)

An enthusiastic piece about one of the great songwriters, published in *Words & Music* in July 2001.

THE PROFESSOR OF POPULAR SONG

Otto Harbach invented the literary lyric

'Smoke Gets in Your Eyes' is one of the outstandingly beautiful songs of all time. It was written for the 1933 Broadway show, *Roberta*, set in a Paris fashion house owned and staffed by Russian emigrés. For the Beatles, it was a model of how a song should be written.

It's supposed to be based on an old Russian proverb, but it comes over as a rueful personal statement, expressed in very delicate language. The smoothly flowing lyric to Jerome Kern's immortal melody was written by Otto Harbach. It represents the last flowering of his long songwriting career.

Harbach might aptly be described as the grandfather of all the great lyric-writers of the golden age of popular song. Born in Salt Lake City in 1873, he came from Danish stock but took his name from the farm on which his impoverished family was employed. Otto worked his way through college, winning the prize for oratory, and became professor of English and public speaking at Whitman College in the state of Washington.

But there wasn't much future in that, so in 1902 he made his way to New York in order to take a master's course at Columbia University, the breeding ground for so many of the leading lyricists. He worked on a newspaper and as an advertising copywriter. He also attended his first Broadway show, and was instantly hooked on the musical theatre.

In 1908 he wrote his first song hit: 'Cuddle Up a Little Closer', followed by the rather daring 'Every Little Movement Has a Meaning all its Own'. The lyric is noteworthy for the little academic flourishes like 'gesture' and 'posture' that Harbach couldn't resist, and which became his individual trademark.

In 1912 he was Rudolf Friml's librettist and lyricist on *The Firefly*, with its lovely waltz song, 'Sympathy'. For the next 25 years Harbach was responsible for the book and lyrics of an enormous number of well-constructed musical plays, working with the leading composers of the day.

At one time he had five plays running simultaneously on Broadway – a feat never equalled before or since. It was he who took the young Oscar Hammerstein II under his wing as a collaborator in the 1920s on such successes as *Rose Marie* ('Indian Love Call'), *The Desert Song* ('One Alone'), and *Sunny* (the delightful 'Who?').

Harbach teamed up with Kern again in 1931 with *The Cat and the Fiddle*, which included the jolly number 'She Didn't Say Yes' as well as the lush romanticism of 'The Night was Made for Love', with its striking image of 'a night without love' being like 'caressing an empty glove'.

Roberta wasn't a great success until the popular crooner, Rudy Vallee, sang 'Smoke Gets in Your Eyes' and the show took off. Harbach's love of language comes through in phrases like 'laughing friends deride' and his rhyming of 'chaffed' with 'laughed'.

Another superb song in the show was 'Yesterdays'. Only a literary genius could have thought up that incredible rhyme 'sequestered days'; and there's a neat triple of 'youth' and 'truth' leading up to 'forsooth'. It's certainly archaic, but in its context it has an old world charm.

It is almost unbelievable that a man with Harbach's record of achievement in the musical theatre should have received so little recognition from historians. He took both book and lyrics out of the Edwardian era, through the First World War and into the liberated Twenties. He had a particularly strong influence on the style of lyric-writing, transforming the stilted language of operetta into idiomatic contemporary speech, without sacrificing the poetical quality of his verse.

Alan Jay Lerner described an incident when Harbach was in his late eighties and in poor health. He told his son Bill that he'd been unable to sleep because he had suddenly realised what was wrong with the lyric of 'Smoke Gets in

Your Eyes'. The fact that time had already decided there was nothing wrong with the lyric was beside the point. Otto Harbach remained a perfectionist to his last breath. He died in 1963, venerated by the lyricists who succeeded him.

This article celebrating the centenary of an 'unknown' lyricist was published in *Words & Music* in September 2001.

A MEMORY TO BE THANKFUL FOR

Leo Robin earned ten Academy Award nominations

'Thanks for the Memory', the hit song of the Hollywood musical *The Big Broadcast* of 1938, became famous as Bob Hope's signature tune, and it has been used countless times as the title of nostalgic radio programmes and showbiz reminiscences. The music was composed by Ralph Rainger and the very clever lyric is by Leo Robin.

It's a sophisticated duet sung by a couple once married, now separated, who meet by chance on an ocean liner. Robin does not celebrate a grand passion, but takes a wrily affectionate look at life in the 1930s for a well-off intelligent couple. The characters may sound flippant and blasé, but you sense that deep down they are still in love with each other, and dare not say it. Therein lies the heartache, and it's an extraordinary achievement to convey that depth of feeling in the lyric of a popular song.

Incidentally, the lyric originally contained the line: 'That weekend at Niagara when we never saw the Falls'. The Paramount censor objected to this as being too suggestive, and changed it to 'when we hardly saw the Falls'. In Robin's view this made the innuendo even worse, but that's the way it came out.

Leo Robin was born in Pittsburgh in 1900 and studied law at the University there. But his heart was in the theatre. He earned his living as a newspaper reporter and publicity agent while trying to establish himself as a playwright. Then George S. Kaufman, the great play doctor, looked at his stuff and advised him to try songwriting.

He finally broke into show business in 1925 when his work was included in a Broadway musical. Two years later he had his first big hit with the lyric for 'Hallelujah' in *Hit the*

Deck. There's a hint of his innovative style in the line: 'Satan lies a-waitin' and creatin' Hell to pay'.

When the talkies came along he was a natural choice for Hollywood, and signed up with Paramount Pictures. In 1929 his song 'Louise' became the personal trademark of the great French entertainer, Maurice Chevalier. I like the skilful way that Robin handles language, and his deft use of internal rhymes. It also takes a lot of skill to write words for a foreign singer performing in English.

For the film *Monte Carlo* he wrote a nice little song called 'Beyond the Blue Horizon' for Jeanette MacDonald to sing to the rhythm of the wheels of a speeding train – simple words, but exactly what you would expect the character to say in such a situation, and quite memorable.

Robin teamed up with the piano player Ralph Rainger in 1932 in a partnership which lasted ten years until his friend's early death in a plane crash. Their first effort together was for the film *The Big Broadcast*, in which Bing Crosby made his debut as a featured player. In the song 'Please', Robin again shows his skill with internal rhymes, slipping them in without interrupting the smooth flow of the music. Here's a good example:

> Your eyes reveal that you have the soul of
> An angel white as snow;
> How long must I play the role of
> A gloomy Romeo?

'Love in Bloom', adopted by Jack Benny as his signature tune, and 'June in January' are just two more fine lyrics from his prolific pen as a Hollywood lyricist.

In 1949 he returned to the New York theatre to work with Julie Styne on one of the most successful musicals, *Gentlemen Prefer Blondes*. This produced some of his best work, including the marvellous 'Diamonds Are a Girl's Best Friend', which must rank high in the table of witty songs, with its audacious rhyming of 'pear-shape' with 'their shape'.

What I like about Robin's work is the sheer fluency of

every lyric – the words just flow on from line to line, and the only time you get a full pause is at the end of the verse. His rhyming is exquisite, and his use of language is masterly. He is able to slip from poetical to colloquial, from serious to humorous, with here and there a striking phrase like 'June in January' that has passed into the language.

Leo Robin died in 1984. This was the man whose songs received ten Academy Award nominations. Justice was finally done when he won the Oscar in 1938 for 'Thanks for the Memory'. Of all his 345 film songs, that is indeed the one he will always be remembered for.

An offshoot from my researches into lyric-writing.

TERSE VERSE

The English language is unique in the number of single-syllable words – nouns, verbs, adjectives, adverbs, pronouns, prepositions, conjunctions. This is because the language is not inflected in the way that other European tongues are. The result is a lyric-writer's dream; he/she can make free with short words to express romantic thoughts in great simplicity.

One of the most unlikely achievements in monosyllabic verse is by that master of polysyllabic rhymes, Lorenz Hart. In the refrain of 'My Heart Stood Still' (1927) the first two verses are written in monosyllables, very skilfully giving the impression of a heart thumping. In the remainder of the lyric he allows himself six words of two syllables. Although he might have found alternatives to single, spoken, unfelt, never, until and moment, it would have sounded very awkward – for example:

> Though not a word of love was said then
> I could tell you knew;
> The way you clasped my hand
> Told me how well you knew.
> I had not lived at all
> Till that great thrill
> Of the first time that
> My heart stood still.

But perhaps the finest example of terse verse is 'I'll Get By' (1928). For this song Roy Turk created a lyric of 46 words using only two words of more than one syllable: darkness and complain. A slight adjustment to the two lines in which these words appear would have completed the record, something like this:

> Though there be rain
> And dark clouds too,
> I'll bear the pain,
> I'll see it through.

186

Another piece prompted by a study of lyric-writers, published in
Words & Music in January 2002.

LYRICAL ECHOES

Lyricists are bound to be influenced by what their contemporaries are writing, so it's not surprising that they occasionally echo one another. Noel Coward's 'A Room with a View'
(*This Year of Grace*, 1928) is reminiscent of Larry Hart's 'The
Blue Room' (*The Girl Friend*, 1926). Hart returned the
compliment with his 'There's a Small Hotel' (*On Your Toes*,
1936), which has echoes of Coward's 'Dear Little Café'
(*Bitter Sweet*, 1929).

Coward's masterpiece, 'If Love Were All', also from *Bitter
Sweet*, has a unique format in that each line of the first verse
rhymes with its counterpart in the second and third verses,
providing a marvellous unity throughout the lyric. Cole
Porter may have recalled this when he used a similar scheme
in 'I Concentrate on You' (in the film *Broadway Melody* of
1940). The two songwriters were great friends, and Coward's
'Nina' in *Sigh No More* (1945) affectionately poked fun at
Porter's epic 'Begin the Beguine' (*Jubilee*, 1935):

> She declined to begin the beguine
> Though they besought her to,
> And in language profane and obscene
> She cursed the man who taught her to,
> She cursed Cole Porter too!

The great Alan Jay Lerner wrote both book and lyrics for *My
Fair Lady* in 1956. In one of Eliza's songs, 'Just You Wait!',
she expresses her exasperation with Professor Higgins by
imagining a time when she is so famous that she can ask the
King for 'Enry 'Iggins' 'ead. Her wish is willingly granted,
and she gleefully supervises his execution by firing squad.

Now Lerner, who had worked with Kurt Weill on *Love Life*
in 1947, was a great admirer of Weill and Brecht's *The*

Threepenny Opera (1928), which he called 'one of the great works of the modern musical theatre'. There's a scene in it where Jenny, the drab dishwasher in a seedy hotel who is abused and insulted by all, imagines herself as a pirate chief whose ship bombards the port and takes prisoner all those who mistreated her. They are led on the ship and executed one by one, with her shouting 'Hopla' as each head falls. Could it be that Lerner, who saw the first Broadway production of *The Threepenny Opera* in 1954, had the story of Pirate Jenny in mind when he created Eliza's song in 1956?

Gus Kahn went back much further, to the 18th-century poets Charles Churchill and William Cowper (contemporaries at Westminster and both writing about England), when he used the line 'With all your faults I love you still' in 'It Had to be You' (1924). This splendidly laconic lyric, written to the music of band-leader Isham Jones, has been used again and again in Hollywood movies, most appropriately in the biopic of Kahn, *I'll See You in My Dreams* (1952).

SONGS

FIRST AND LAST SONGS

After I retired, a study of the lyric-writers in the golden age of popular song between the wars led me into the field of music. Between 1994 and 2000 I composed ten songs in various idioms, which were published individually by DaCapo Music Ltd.

One is based on a favourite poem by C. Day Lewis, by kind permission of the poet's widow. She told me that the subject of 'The Unwanted' is the provenance of a poem or other work of art, where the artist's preferred choice may be rejected in favour of a possibly inferior one.

The remaining songs have my own lyrics, with 'A Shropshire Lass' being set to the music of Schubert's 'Trout'.

As I am not a musician and have no knowledge of harmony, the melodies are simple and place few demands on the singer. They are therefore more suited to amateur than professional singers.

The 'Hymn to the Arts' has been sung by church choirs in Bromley's annual Service for the Arts. 'Beneath the Bajan Moon' has proved popular with amateur groups, as has 'Spring Weather', which is usually sung in French and English consecutively. 'Flying Fish' has been used by a local music teacher, and sung once in concert.

A SIMPLE SONGBOOK

1.	'Hymn to the Arts'	Festival Song
2.	'Beneath the Bajan Moon'	Edwardian Ballad
3.	'I Can't Get Fat Like Father'	Victorian Music Hall
4.	'Seven Days of Loving'	Rock/Show Song
5.	'The Unwanted'	Folk Song
6.	'Flying Fish'	Caribbean Calypso
7.	'Queen of My Heart'	Country & Western
8.	'Spring Weather'	Georgian Rondeau
9.	'Bromley Blues'	New Orleans Style
10.	'A Shropshire Lass'	Art Song

Hymn To The Arts

a festival song for accompanied voices

Words and melody by Roy Dean
Music arranged by Christopher Field

Voices

Piano / Organ

1.Praise the paint - ers who de - light the eye,——— Praise the sing - ers rais - ing voi - ces high;———
2.Praise the sculp - tors carv - ing wood and stone,——— Praise com - po - sers blend - ing tune and tone;———

Praise mus - i - cians mak - ing joy— ful noise,——— Praise the dan - cers with their
Praise the play - wrights set - ting scene— on scene,——— Praise di - rec - tors on the

grace and poise.____ Praise the po - ets who en - rich our hearts,____
stage and screen.____ Praise the nov - el - ists whose writ - ing thrills,____

Praise the ac - tors play - ing ma__ ny parts;____ Praise the ma - kers of our
Praise the crafts - men for their sub__ tle skills;____ Praise the arch - i - tects who

fest__ i - val,____ And praise the Lord who made them all.
built__ our hall,____ And praise the Lord who made them all.

Beneath The Bajan Moon

for mezzo-soprano (or baritone) and piano

Words and music: Roy Dean
Piano arrangement: Janet Bishop

Slowly, with feeling

At close of day the palm trees sway, As

shad - ows fall on still lag - oon; A spi - cy breeze car - ess - es trees Be-

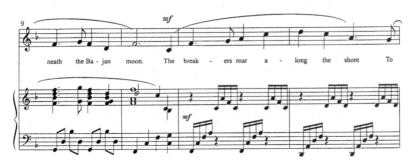

neath the Ba - jan moon. The break - ers roar a - long the shore To

195

surge and shim - mer on the dune; The tro - pic night is bathed in light Be-

neath the Ba - jan moon. Mag - ic is - land of Bar - bad - os,

Safe from tem - pests and tor - na - dos, May your beau - ty ev - er be

I Can't Get Fat Like Father

for baritone and piano

Words and Music: Roy Dean
Piano arrangement: Janet Bishop

198

keep my dain-ty fig-ure. Fa - ther! Fa - ther! I can't get fat like fa-ther.

Fa - ther! Fa - ther! I'd like to be like Dad. Though beer tastes good, with-out a doubt, It

has-n't got the la-ther; So I drink stout to blow me out, But I can't get fat like fa-ther. The

oth - er night the mayor came in To have his week- ly ton- ic. He mur - mured as he sipped his gin "My

in - dig- est- ion's chro - nic. Al - though in limb I'm ve - ry sound The wind gives me dam - na - tion; I'd

glad- ly give a thou- sand pound To have your cor- por- a - tion". Fa- ther! Fa- ther! He

Chorus

can't get fat like fa-ther. Fa-ther! Fa-ther! He wants to be like Dad. He

al-ways drinks a glass of gin Be - cause, you see, he'd ra-ther; But drink-ing gin just keeps him thin And he

can't get fat like fa - ther.

Seven Days of Loving

for tenor and piano

Words & music: Roy Dean
Piano arrangement: Janet Bishop

Moderate tempo:
(strong rhythm)

Voice

Piano

We had our hon-ey-moon,— we saw the tour-ist sights.— We loved the

sun-ny days—— and loved the star-ry nights.— I tried to keep in shape.— like an-y

fit-ness freak,— But ba-by, sev-en days of lov-ing—— make— one weak.——

202

We were a lov - ing cou— ple at the lov - ing cup,— We nev - er

thought the nec— tar would be all used up.— Al - though I used to think— I had a

strong phy-sique,— I know that sev - en days of lov-ing make— one weak.— Oh why

is my strength re- ced - ing when I'm need- ing all I've got? Oh why

is my blood con - geal - ing when the feel- ing should be hot? You might as

well switch off,___ it is - n't an - y use,___ The mo - tor can - not start___ be - cause it's

out of juice.___ I'm ve - ry sad to say___ I must have passed my peak___ When on - ly

sev - en days of lov - ing___ make___ one weak.___ Now my head is split - ting___

I don't mind ad - mit - ting___ Se - ven days of lov - ing___ make___ one weak.

The Unwanted

(poem: C. Day Lewis)
for tenor (or soprano) and piano

Music: Roy Dean
Piano arrangement: Janet Bishop

On a day when the breath of ro- ses Plump-ened a swoon- ing breeze, And all the sil - ken combes of sum- mer Op - ened wide their knees, Be - tween two sighs they

plan - ted one, A willed one, a wan - ted one, And he will be the

sign, they said, Of our fel - i - ci - ties. Ea - ger the loins he sprang from,——

Hap-py the shelt' ring heart; Sel - dom had the seed of man So

charmed, so clear a start. And he was born as frail a one, So

ail - ing, freak - ish, pale a one, As e - ver the wry plan——— ets

(sombre)

Knot- ted their beams to thwart. Sun locked up for win- ter;

L. V.

Earth an emp-ty rind; Two strang-ers harsh-ly flung tog - eth - er As by a flail of

wind. Oh was it not a furt - ive thing, A love - less, damned, ab - ort - ive thing - This flur - ry of the

groan-ing dust And what it left be - hind! Sure, from such warped beg - inn - ings

sempre legato

No-thing deb-on-air Can come? But nei-ther shame nor pan-ic, Drugs nor sharp des-pair Could up-root that un-to-ward thing That all too fierce and fro-ward thing; Wil-ly-nil-ly born it was, Div-ine-ly formed and fair. Div-ine-ly formed and fair.

Flying Fish

for contralto and piano

Words and music: Roy Dean
Piano arrangement: Janet Bishop

Calypso rhythm

Down in Bridge-town there's a lit - tle har - bour,—

Where the fish - er-men land,———— Ev - 'ry eve-ning you can hear them call-ing,—

With their catch— in their hand. Buy, Oh buy— me love-ly fly - ing fish.———

Try, Oh try— them, they are quite de-lish;——— Fry, oh fry— them an - y way you wish,———

My, oh my— they're such a tas - ty dish.———

Crowds of peo-ple all a - long the quay— side,— Come to hag - gle and buy;———

High a - bove all the noi - sy rum - pus,— Hear the fish— er men cry.

Buy, Oh buy— me love- ly fly - ing fish.— Try, Oh try— them, they are quite de- lish;—

Fry, oh fry— them an- y way you wish,— My, oh my— they're such a tas - ty dish.—

Queen of my Heart

for baritone and piano

Words and music: Roy Dean
Piano arrangement: Janet Bishop

Slowly, with feeling

Voice

Piano

I've lost my dear

wife Who's the love of my life; She'll al - ways be queen of my

heart._____ Through good times and bad She would make me feel

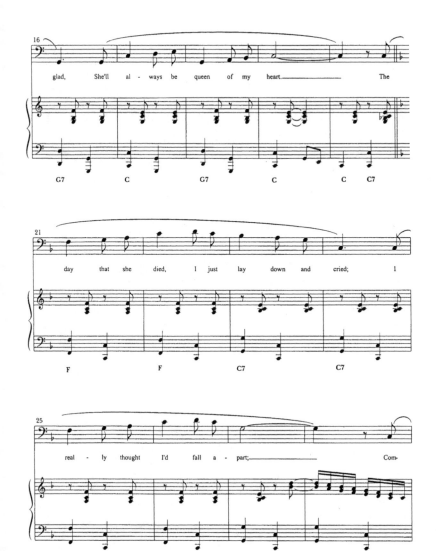

Spring Weather

French text: Charles d'Orléans (1394-1465)

for baritone and piano

Words and Music: Roy Dean
Piano arrangement: Janet Bishop

Old weath-er's shed his som-bre shroud Of wind and
Le temps a laiss - ié son man - teau De vent, de

rain and bit-ter cold, And let his broi - de-ry un-fold Of shin-ing sun - light clear and
froi - dure et de pluye, Et s'est ves-tu de brou-de - rie, De sol-eil luy - ant, cler et

proud. The birds and beasts all sing a-loud, Each giv-ing tongue in his own mould; Old weath-er's
beau. Il n'y a best - e, ne oy - seau Qu'en son jar - gon ne chant ou crie; Le temps a

217

shed   his som-bre   shroud   Of wind and   rain and bit-ter   cold.   Riv-er and stream   and foun-tain
laiss - ié son man - teau   De vent, de   froi-dure et de   pluye.   Riv-ièr -. e,   fon - taine et ruiss-

loud   Are wear-ing as   their liv-ery bold   Jew-els of sil - ver and of gold,   All is with rai - ment new en-
eau   Port-ent, en liv - ré-e jo - lie,   Goutt-es d'ar-gent   d'or-fav-rer- ie,   Chas-cun s'a - bill - e de nou-

dowed.   Old weath-er's shed   his som-bre   shroud.
veau.   Le temps a   laiss - ié son man - teau.

218

Bromley Blues

for contralto and piano

Words and music: Roy Dean
Piano arrangement: Janet Bishop

I feel so mis-'ra-ble,—— I

got - ta get out of town. Yeah, I'm so

mis-'ra-ble,—— I wan-na—— leave—— this—— town.——

219

'Cause the man I love,——— he's gone and let me down.—

E♭m   E♭m7   E♭m   E♭m   B♭7

——— We loved so sweet-ly,——— could-n't

E♭m   E♭m7   E♭m   E♭m7   G   C7

bear to be a-part.——— Used to love so sweet-ly,———

C7   Fm   F7   Fm   F7   B♭   B♭7

220

We could - n't be a - part._____ But he

B♭   B♭7   E♭m   E♭m7   E♭m   E♭m7

walked out on me,_____ And broke my poor old heart._____

E♭m   E♭m   B♭7   E♭m   E♭m7

One of these morn-ings,_____ I'm gon-na_____ catch that train.

E♭m   E♭m7 G   C7   C7   Fm   F7

221

To-mor-row morn-ing,—— I'll be on that train.——

Fm   F7   B♭   B♭7   B♭   B♭7   E♭m   E♭m7

And this old town—— won't see my face a - gain,——

E♭m   E♭m7   E♭m   E♭m   B♭7   E♭m   E♭m7

won't see my face a - gain.——   won't see my face a - gain.——

E♭m   B♭   E♭m   E♭m7   E♭m   B♭   E♭m

A Shropshire Lass

(to die for elle)

Words: Roy Dean
Music: F. Schubert

Tenor

Piano

p legato

1.In spring, the hawthorn scat - ters Its
2.Her mouth was soft and will - ing, Her

pp

p

snow a - long the hedge, And thoughts of coun try mat - ters Run
eyes were like the sea: I off - ered her a shil - ling If

223

CROSSWORD AND QUIZ ANSWERS

THE APOSTROPHE GAME

1. HARRIET BEECHER'S TOW
2. WALTER'S COT
3. GERTRUDE'S TINE
4. IRVING'S TONE
5. MIKHAIL'S HOLLOW-COUGH
6. LAURENCE'S TURN
7. SAM'S PAID
8. NEVIL'S HOOT
9. BERNARD'S WHORE
10. ADAM'S MYTH
11. FORSYTE'S AGA
12. MILES'S TAN DISH
13. CECIL'S HARP
14. STEPHEN'S ON TIME
15. GEORGE'S TUBS
16. MALCOLM'S ARGENT
17. ROLLING'S TONES
18. MUNTHE'S UNDIES
19. SOMETHING'S TURD
20. MAIDEN'S PEACH
21. KITCHEN'S INK
22. MATERNITY'S MOCK
23. PUBLIC'S COOL
24. WIFE'S WHOPPING
25. CORK'S CREW
26. JOCK'S TRAP
27. BAND'S TANNED
28. HEAD'S TART
29. GUM'S HEALED
30. BEAUTY'S POT
31. POTTING'S HEAD
32. SWEEP'S TAKE
33. OIL'S LICK
34. INN'S WINGER
35. CROP'S PRAYER
36. APRIL'S HOURS

MUSIC IN THE SQUARE

```
S O N D H E I M
O P E R E T T A
N E N U P H A R
D R U M S E L L
H E P S A R I A
E T H E R C A P
I T A L I A N S
M A R L A P S E
```

FIND THE PAINTER

1. Leonardo da Vinci
2. Claude Monet
3. Francis Bacon
4. John Constable
5. Sandro Botticelli
6. Albrecht Durer
7. Piero della Francesca
8. Paul Klee
9. David Hockney
10. Ivon Hitchens
11. Edgar Degas
12. Georges Seurat
13. Andy Warhol
14. Jan Vermeer
15. Andrew Wyeth
16. Auguste Renoir
17. Andrea Mantegna
18. Samuel Palmer
19. Henri Matisse
20. Salvador Dali
21. Pieter Brueghel
22. Pablo Picasso
23. Paul Nash
24. Stanley Spencer
25. Lucian Freud

MOZART MEDLEY

1. *Le Nozze di Figaro*
2. 'Exsultate Jubilate'
3. 'Das Veilchen'
4. Bassoon Concerto
5. *Don Giovanni*
6. Sinfonia Concertante
7. *Cosi Fan Tutte*
8. 'Haffner' Serenade
9. *Die Zauberflöte*
10. Rondo in A Minor
11. *Eine Kleine Nachtmusik*
12. Clarinet Quintet
13. *La Clemenza di Tito*
14. Minuet in D
15. Symphony in G Minor
16. 'Jupiter' Symphony
17. *Musikalischer Spass*
18. *Serenata Notturna*
19. Requiem Mass
20. 'Hunt' Quartet

CLOSING THE VOWELS

1. Armouries
2. Auctioned
3. Auriscope
4. Authorise
5. Autocrime
6. Autopsies
7. Autotimer
8. Behaviour
9. Cautioned
10. Cointreau
11. Education
12. Emulation
13. Equivocal
14. Euphorbia
15. Exudation
16. Favourite
17. Foliature
18. Housemaid
19. Inoculate
20. Jailhouse
21. Labourite
22. Nefarious
23. Odalisque
24. Ossuaries
25. Outsailed
26. Pneumonia
27. Savouries
28. Tenacious
29. Veracious
30. Vexatious

CRYPTIC CROSSWORD CLUES

[Anag. = anagram, rev. = reversed, & lit. = the whole clue is a literal definition of the answer]

1. AVIATORS [A-VIA-TORS, & lit.]

2. PALISADES [Sounds like 'Palace Aides'].

3. SIGNIFICANT [SIGN-IF-I-CAN'T, i.e. if I'm not back in time, said by boss dictating letter].

4. SHERIDAN [Author of *The School for Scandal*].

5. ANNIVERSARY [Anag.].

6. MAN-MANAGEMENT [MAN-MAN-AGE-MEN-T(ackle)].

7. DOLCE VITA [Anag., ref. 'Bet your sweet life', & lit.].

8. CHRISTMAS BOX [Anag. + BOX = strike].

9. REFRIGERATOR [REF-RIG-ERA-TO-R (= run)].

10. FEMME FATALE [ME(N)-FAT in FEMALE, & lit.]

11. INCANDESCENT [INCAN-DESCENT].

12. FEMININE ENDING [Double meaning, E = Grammatical term, or Ecstasy, & lit].

13. CANDLELIGHT [Anag., & lit].

14. BERLIOZ [Sounds like 'Barely owes'].

15. IRIS MURDOCH [CO(NUN)DRUM rev. in IRISH].

16. FORD MADOX FORD [FORD-MAD-OXFORD].

17. SMOKING [KIN in SMOG, & lit.]

18. UNYIELDING [Double meaning].

19. LATERALLY [LATE-RALLY].

20. ATTITUDINISE [Anag., & lit.]

21. INFESTATION [Anag., & lit].

22. TERPSICHOREAN [Anag., & lit].

23. CABARET [BARE in anag. of ACT, & lit].

24. MOTHERS-IN-LAW [Anag. minus O, & lit].

25. LIFELINE [L-I-FELINE, & lit].

26. SPEAKEASY [PEAK in SEAS-Y].

27. DRESSING-ROOM [hidden].

28. COCKPIT [2 double meanings].

29. RECORD [Hole fits on spindle of player].

30. PANICKING [(HIS)PANIC KING].

31. MITTERRAND [MITT-ERRAND].

32. EVEN NUMBER [2 double meanings].

33. ADMINISTRATE [AD-MINIS-T-RATE].

34. IN CAHOOTS [INCA HOOTS].

35. PLEASANTRY [L in PEASANTRY].

36. INSPECTOR MORSE [Anag. & lit].

37. CHARLES IVES [Anag. of EARL'S in CHIVES].

38. PORTRAITURE [OR = Soldiers + TRAIT in PURE, & lit].

39. ESTATE CAR [hidden].

40. SONG THRUSH [Anag.].

41. NOUGHTS [Anag.].

42. BISTRO [initials of clue words].

43. SEASCAPES (3 double meanings].

44. PRODIGAL SON [PRO-DIG-ALSO-N].

45. DOWNSIDE [Double meaning].

46. NEW YEAR'S EVE (Anag., & lit].

47. POST OFFICE [2 double meanings].

48. LEG-OVER [EG in LOVER, & lit].

49. SAL VOLATILE [SALVO + sound of LATTERLY].

50. HANG-GLIDER [Anag minus H, & lit]